CONTEMPORARY TOPICS 3

ADVANCED LISTENING AND NOTE-TAKING SKILLS

SECOND EDITION

DAVID BEGLAR

NEIL MURRAY

MICHAEL ROST
SERIES EDITOR

longman.com

Contemporary Topics 3: Advanced Listening and Note-Taking Skills, Second Edition, Teacher's Pack
Copyright © 2002 by Pearson Education, Inc.
All rights reserved.

Pearson Education, 10 Bank Street, White Plains, NY 10606

Vice president, publishing: Allen Ascher
Senior acquisitions editor: Ginny Blanford
Development director: Penny Laporte
Development editor: Lise Minovitz
Vice president, director of design and production: Rhea Banker
Executive managing editor: Linda Moser
Production manager: Ray Keating
Production editor: Michael Mone
Director of manufacturing: Patrice Fraccio
Senior manufacturing buyer: Dave Dickey
Cover design: Rainbow Graphics
Text composition: Rainbow Graphics

ISBN: 0-13-094865-9

Printed in the United States of America
3 4 5 6 7 8 9 10–DPC–05 04 03

CONTENTS

INTRODUCTION

The materials in this pack provide additional resources for you, the teacher, to meet the needs of your classroom. Included are photocopiable unit quizzes, audioscripts and answer keys for the unit quizzes, answer keys for selected Student Book exercises, and lecture audioscripts.

Although the lectures and activities in *Contemporary Topics* provide the basis for learning, the key to making this program work in the classroom is, as always, involvement. Listening is an active process that involves predicting, guessing, interacting, risk-taking, clarifying, questioning, and responding. The authors and editors of *Contemporary Topics* hope that they have created a rich framework for making students more active, successful learners—and for encouraging you to be a more active guide in that process.

THE UNIT QUIZZES

The unit quizzes on pages 1 through 12 may be photocopied for use with students in a classroom. These quizzes not only give students an opportunity to see what they have learned, they also provide useful opportunities for TOEFL®-style test-taking practice. Each unit quiz consists of two parts. Part A assesses students' listening comprehension and understanding of the lecture with six multiple-choice questions. Part B assesses students' ability to reconstruct and restate information from the lecture as they provide written responses to two open-ended questions. Taking these quizzes familiarizes students with how to approach multiple-choice and written exam questions, something they need to practice in order to succeed in their university work.

Administering the unit quiz shortly after completing the unit helps train students to recall information. Depending on the goals of your course and your students' needs, you may want to consider the following questions.

- Do you want to emphasize test-taking strategies? If so, encouraging your students to study their notes at home and timing the quizzes simulates an academic testing situation.
- Do you want to emphasize note-taking strategies? If so, letting your students use their notes during the quiz promotes effective study skills.

Answers for the multiple-choice questions in the unit quizzes are provided in the answer keys that follow each quiz. In addition, possible answers for the open-ended questions are supplied. These are intended as sample answers; individual responses may vary.

Other Assessment Techniques

Effective assessment is an integral part of any course. It helps you evaluate what the students know and the areas in which they need more help. In addition to using the unit quizzes, you may want to use the assessment techniques below.

- Ask students to review their notes from a lecture they heard several classes earlier, and then give them a short, open-response question similar to those in the unit quiz.
- Give vocabulary quizzes, reviewing the words from earlier units. This can be done as a spelling quiz, a fill-in-the-blank activity, or a sentence-writing activity.
- Have students create vocabulary quizzes for each other. They can create the quizzes at home or in class.
- Have students create quizzes for each other based on the content of the lectures. Share responses within the class.

STUDENT BOOK ANSWER KEYS

Answers are provided for many exercises in the Vocabulary Preview and Listen to the Lecture sections of each unit. In addition, answers are provided for some Taking Better Notes and Using Your Notes sections. Where students are asked to write a sentence or brief essay, sample answers are provided for your convenience.

The Student Book activities that accompany each lecture are designed to slow down the listening process. Students are encouraged to preview vocabulary, listen with a clear purpose, take notes efficiently, organize and review their notes, and apply the content. The activities also help students develop critical thinking skills, including:

- activating prior knowledge
- guessing meaning from context
- predicting information
- organizing ideas
- discriminating between main ideas and details
- reconstructing and summarizing main ideas
- transferring knowledge from lectures to other areas

LECTURE AUDIOSCRIPTS

Each level of the *Contemporary Topics* series comprises twelve original lectures on relevant contemporary topics drawn from a range of academic disciplines, accessible to students of all backgrounds. The audioscripts for all lectures are included here so that you can have a clear record of what your students have heard. You can use the audioscripts to prepare for presentation of the lecture.

One of the key features of the new *Contemporary Topics* series is the authentic sound of the recorded lectures. Lecturers hesitate, add discourse markers, ask questions of their students, and are interrupted by student questions in turn. Our intent was to give your students practice with a classroom experience that is as realistic and natural as possible, while still ensuring that the lectures are comprehensible. The audioscripts included here reflect all of this, with pauses represented by ellipses. Please note that these audioscripts are included as a resource for you and should not be read aloud to the class, since this would create a more artificial lecture than is available on the audiocassettes or audio CDs.

LONGMAN ON THE WEB

Longman.com offers classroom activities, teaching tips, and online resources for teachers of all levels and students of all ages. Visit us for course-specific Companion Websites, our comprehensive online catalogue of all Longman titles, and access to all local Longman websites, offices, and contacts around the world.

Join a global community of teachers and students at Longman.com.

Longman English Success offers online courses to give learners flexible, self-paced study options. Developed for distance learning or to complement classroom instruction, courses cover General English, Business English, and Exam Preparation.

For more information visit EnglishSuccess.com.

UNIT 1 QUIZ

A Listen to each question. Circle the letter of the correct answer.

1. a. Casual language used by particular communities
   b. Unacceptable language used by subcultures
   c. Language used by criminal organizations

2. a. It makes them feel important.
   b. It gives them an identity.
   c. It has strong negative meanings.

3. a. In formal situations
   b. In informal situations
   c. In formal and informal situations

4. a. It's fashionable.
   b. It's fun.
   c. It challenges authority.

5. a. Positive and negative feelings
   b. Love and romance
   c. School and work

6. a. They're unacceptable in many subcultures.
   b. People become bored with them.
   c. They're associated with famous personalities.

B Answer each question. Use complete sentences.

1. How does slang help construct and cement group identity?

_____
_____
_____
_____

2. How is the use of slang today different from its use in the seventeenth century?

_____
_____
_____
_____

UNIT 2 QUIZ

A **Listen to each question. Circle the letter of the correct answer.**

1. **a.** The best-laid plans of mice and men often go awry.
   b. Anything that can go wrong will go wrong.
   c. The line next to you will move faster than yours.

2. **a.** About 0 percent
   b. About 50 percent
   c. About 100 percent

3. **a.** It affects the speed.
   b. It affects the weight.
   c. It affects the rate of spin.

4. **a.** The laws of physics
   b. Probability theory
   c. Random behavior

5. **a.** A flower
   b. The weather
   c. Dice

6. **a.** A gambler's fallacy
   b. A life history
   c. A single-event probability

B **Answer each question. Use complete sentences.**

1. What mathematical formula determines your chances of choosing the fastest supermarket line? Write the formula and explain it.

   _____

   _____

   _____

   _____

2. Define the gambler's fallacy. Give one example.

   _____

   _____

   _____

   _____

UNIT 3 QUIZ

A **Listen to each question. Circle the letter of the correct answer.**

1. **a.** By main ideas or details
   b. By the senses used
   c. By duration

2. **a.** Less than half a second
   b. Two seconds or less
   c. About a minute

3. **a.** When sleeping
   b. When reading
   c. When hearing sounds

4. **a.** Less than one second
   b. Between one and two seconds
   c. Five to ten seconds

5. **a.** It specializes in holding meaning.
   b. It loses much information.
   c. It registers impressions.

6. **a.** The recall test
   b. The recognition test
   c. The memorization test

B **Answer each question. Use complete sentences.**

1. What three types of memory were discussed in the lecture? Describe one of them.

   _____

   _____

   _____

   _____

2. What three ways of measuring memory were discussed in the lecture? Describe one of them.

   _____

   _____

   _____

   _____

UNIT 4 QUIZ

A Listen to each question. Circle the letter of the correct answer.

1. **a.** Body language
   b. Physical contact
   c. Creative expressions

2. **a.** About 25 percent
   b. About 50 percent
   c. About 75 percent

3. **a.** G. W. Porter
   b. Richard Nixon
   c. Raymond Birdwhistle

4. **a.** Physical, symbolic, aesthetic, and signs
   b. Physical, static, dynamic, and intimate
   c. Physical, dynamic, aesthetic, and kinesic

5. **a.** Eye contact
   b. Distance
   c. Posture

6. **a.** People can't clarify or repeat it.
   b. Its grammar is the same in every culture.
   c. We can control it better.

B Answer each question. Use complete sentences.

1. Why do we need to be careful about gestures? Give examples.

   _____

   _____

   _____

   _____

2. How has research on body language been helpful in business? Give examples.

   _____

   _____

   _____

   _____

UNIT 5 QUIZ

A Listen to each question. Circle the letter of the correct answer.

1. **a.** Caring for children
   b. Working full-time
   c. Social development of the parents

2. **a.** Children's financial security
   b. Children's social development
   c. Children's education

3. **a.** It is more common.
   b. It is not biased.
   c. It is accepted by society.

4. **a.** Young people choose marriage partners independently.
   b. Families choose marriage partners.
   c. Some countries have made it illegal.

5. **a.** It is becoming more common.
   b. It is becoming less common.
   c. It is becoming illegal in some countries.

6. **a.** More international marriages
   b. Larger families
   c. More arranged marriages

B Answer each question. Use complete sentences.

1. Write one definition of marriage provided by the speaker. Give an example.

   _____

   _____

   _____

   _____

2. Write a definition of endogamy. Give an example.

   _____

   _____

   _____

   _____

UNIT 6 QUIZ

A **Listen to each question. Circle the letter of the correct answer.**

1. **a.** They can see their effects on nearby objects.
   b. They have mathematical proof of their existence.
   c. White dwarfs have proof of their existence.

2. **a.** A very old compressed star
   b. A very new large star
   c. The center of a white hole

3. **a.** Its heat, energy, and mass are compressed into a smaller space.
   b. Its heat, energy, and mass increase rapidly.
   c. Its gravitational force becomes much weaker.

4. **a.** Mass and heat
   b. Gravity and mass
   c. Heat and gravity

5. **a.** At the center of a black hole
   b. In the area around a black hole
   c. Between the third and fourth dimensions

6. **a.** At the center of a black hole
   b. In the area around a black hole
   c. Between a black hole and a wormhole

B **Answer each question. Use complete sentences.**

1. Why is travel through a wormhole unlikely?

_____

_____

_____

_____

2. How are black holes, white holes, and wormholes connected? Draw a sketch and label it.

UNIT 7 QUIZ

A Listen to each question. Circle the letter of the correct answer.

1. **a.** Symbolic communication
   b. Affective communication
   c. Ultrasonic communication

2. **a.** It runs up a tree.
   b. It scans the sky.
   c. It scans the ground.

3. **a.** Monkeys and birds
   b. Chimpanzees and snakes
   c. Leopards and eagles

4. **a.** Communicating only to male or female chickens
   b. Indicating that food is present when it is not
   c. Becoming quiet when no other chickens are present

5. **a.** Use language to communicate emotion
   b. Use odors to communicate emotion
   c. Use language in a symbolic way

6. **a.** Acquire thousands of words
   b. Communicate with different species
   c. Combine notes in different patterns

B Answer each question. Use complete sentences.

1. Define *referent*. Give an example of an animal using a referent when communicating.

   _____

   _____

   _____

   _____

2. Do animals intend to communicate? Explain.

   _____

   _____

   _____

   _____

UNIT 8 QUIZ

A Listen to each question. Circle the letter of the correct answer.

1. **a.** Women's conversations about work and money
   b. The number of women in the workforce
   c. The amount of time boys and girls play together

2. **a.** The speaker's gender
   b. The speaker's communication style
   c. The speaker's status

3. **a.** 30
   b. 40
   c. 70

4. **a.** 60
   b. 75
   c. 99

5. **a.** Intimacy-related
   b. Collaboration-oriented
   c. Competition-oriented

6. **a.** Women and clothes
   b. Business and money
   c. Food and drink

B Answer each question. Use complete sentences.

1. What factors cause gender differences in communication?

   _____

   _____

   _____

   _____

2. How do typical playtime activities for boys and girls differ?

   _____

   _____

   _____

   _____

UNIT 9 QUIZ

A **Listen to each question. Circle the letter of the correct answer.**

1. **a.** In ancient Egypt
   b. In ancient Greece and Rome
   c. In London's Saville Row

2. **a.** The type, size, and number of garments
   b. The color, number, and type of garments
   c. The color, age, and type of garments

3. **a.** Wearing designer clothes
   b. Wearing expensive materials
   c. Wearing expensive jewelry

4. **a.** Owning many similar garments
   b. Wearing many clothes simultaneously
   c. Wearing only expensive clothing

5. **a.** It's less comfortable than newer materials.
   b. It's becoming extremely scarce.
   c. It's cheap and easy to produce.

6. **a.** Materials are expensive.
   b. Advertising is expensive.
   c. Labor is expensive.

B **Answer each question. Use complete sentences.**

1. What is conspicuous division? Give a definition and an example.

   _____

   _____

   _____

   _____

2. What is conspicuous outrage? Give a definition and an example.

   _____

   _____

   _____

   _____

UNIT 10 QUIZ

A Listen to each question. Circle the letter of the correct answer.

1. a. Extensive practice
 b. Good teachers
 c. Personality characteristics

2. a. People have not yet reached their limits.
 b. People's innate ability is still developing.
 c. Today's athletes are more highly motivated.

3. a. General memory skills
 b. Specialized memory skills
 c. General and specialized memory skills

4. a. They become anxious.
 b. They lose their abilities.
 c. They don't practice.

5. a. 6 years
 b. 10 years
 c. 21 years

6. a. There are too many genetic factors.
 b. Skill development theories are incompatible.
 c. Separating genetic and environmental factors is difficult.

B Answer each question. Use complete sentences.

1. How do social factors contribute to skill development? Give two examples.

_____

_____

_____

_____

2. How does innate talent contribute to skill development? Give two examples.

_____

_____

_____

_____

UNIT 11 QUIZ

A **Listen to each question. Circle the letter of the correct answer.**

1. **a.** The lack of affordable air travel
   b. The introduction of new technology
   c. The global spread of English

2. **a.** Advertising
   b. Technology
   c. Immigration

3. **a.** They are extremely humorous.
   b. They have a lot of advertising.
   c. They are about common human experiences.

4. **a.** Fads
   b. Food
   c. Language

5. **a.** They introduce things from their home cultures.
   b. They change existing political conditions.
   c. They encourage travel to their home cultures.

6. **a.** Materialism and immorality
   b. Prejudice and violence
   c. Inflation and poverty

B **Answer each question. Use complete sentences.**

1. What factors have contributed to the development of a global culture? Give examples.

   _____

   _____

   _____

   _____

2. What are the advantages of a global superculture? Give examples.

   _____

   _____

   _____

   _____

UNIT 12 QUIZ

A Listen to each question. Circle the letter of the correct answer.

1. **a.** 40
   b. 50
   c. 70

2. **a.** A young man
   b. A government agent
   c. A system administrator

3. **a.** By stealing private information
   b. By impersonating other people
   c. By transmitting virus programs

4. **a.** Credit card or social security numbers
   b. Goods, inventory, or sales figures
   c. Government secrets or financial records

5. **a.** Password guessers
   b. Access-control software
   c. Audit trails

6. **a.** Firewalls
   b. Encryption software
   c. System administrators

B Answer each question. Use complete sentences.

1. Why do people engage in computer crime? List the reasons.

   _____
   _____
   _____
   _____

2. Describe a typical hacking scenario.

   _____
   _____
   _____
   _____

UNIT QUIZ AUDIOSCRIPTS AND ANSWER KEYS

Unit 1 Slang: Talking *Cool*

Quiz Audioscript, Part A

1. What is slang?
2. Why do people use slang?
3. When do people use slang?
4. According to the speaker, why is slang *cool*? Circle two answers.
5. What is the most common slang theme?
6. Why do some slang expressions disappear quickly?

Answer Key, Part A

1. a 2. b 3. b 4. a, b 5. a 6. c

Answer Key, Part B

Sample Answers:

1. Slang gives groups of people a private language to enjoy shared experiences and keep everyone else at a distance. Slang is used to express the group's experiences, beliefs, and values.
2. Today, slang is used much more widely. Also, it is no longer associated only with criminals and vagrants.

Unit 2 Murphy's Law

Quiz Audioscript, Part A

1. What is Murphy's Law?
2. What is the probability that toast will fall buttered-side down?
3. How does gravity cause falling toast to land buttered-side down?
4. What affects our chances of choosing the fastest supermarket line?
5. What item does not have a life history?
6. What do statisticians call one roll of a pair of dice?

Answer Key, Part A

1. b 2. c 3. c 4. b 5. c 6. c

Answer Key, Part B

Sample Answers:

1. The formula is 1 ÷ N. The probability of choosing the fastest line is 1 divided by the number of lines (N). For example, if there are three lines, your chances are 1 divided by 3, or 33 percent.
2. The gambler's fallacy is the incorrect belief that gambling devices such as dice have a life history. For example, some gamblers believe if they haven't rolled a seven for some time, they will roll a seven next. However, this is impossible to predict because each roll is independent of the previous rolls.

Unit 3 Types of Memory

Quiz Audioscript, Part A

1. What is a common way to categorize memory?
2. How long does sensory memory last?
3. When is working memory necessary?
4. How long does working memory hold information?
5. What is the essential feature of long-term memory?
6. What test requires you to produce information?

Answer Key, Part A

1. c 2. a 3. b 4. b 5. a 6. a

Answer Key, Part B

Sample Answers:

1. Sensory memory, working memory, and long-term memory were discussed. Long-term memory refers to memories that are stored for long periods of time. Long-term memory specializes in holding meaning; however, the memories may become distorted.
2. Memory can be measured by testing recognition, recall, relearning. In a recognition test, you try to recognize if you have seen or heard something before. An example is looking at a list of ten words one day; the next day you look at another list and try to remember which ten words you saw before.

Unit 4 Actions Speak Louder Than Words

Quiz Audioscript, Part A

1. What does *kinesics* mean?
2. What percentage of communication is nonverbal?
3. Who said that the meaning of nonverbal communication depends on context?
4. What four types of nonverbal communication did G. W. Porter identify?
5. What is an example of dynamic nonverbal communication?
6. How is nonverbal communication different from verbal communication?

Answer Key, Part A

1. a 2. c 3. c 4. a 5. a 6. a

Answer Key, Part B

Sample Answers:

1. The same gestures can have different meanings in different cultures, so we have to be careful how we use them. For example, a circle made with the thumb and first finger means "OK" in the United States, but it has a sexual meaning in South America.
2. Research on body language has been used to improve employees' performance. For example, leaning forward suggests they are energetic and prepared to make changes. Also, standing tall suggests they're good presenters, while taking up a lot of space suggests they're good informers and listeners.

Unit 5 Marriage: Traditions and Trends

Quiz Audioscript, Part A

1. According to the speaker, what is one important marriage obligation?
2. What are fathers traditionally responsible for?
3. Why do some people prefer the term *social parenthood* to *social fatherhood*?
4. What is the key feature of arranged marriages?
5. What is happening to the extended family?
6. What is one possible result of greater exogamy?

Answer Key, Part A

1. a 2. b 3. b 4. b 5. b 6. a

Answer Key, Part B

Sample Answers:

1. The speaker defined marriage as a durable union between one or more men and one or more women. An example is a lasting marriage between one man and one woman.
2. Endogomy is the idea that marriage should take place with someone inside one's group. An example is marrying someone of the same race, nationality, or religion.

Unit 6 Black Holes, White Holes, and Wormholes

Quiz Audioscript, Part A

1. How do scientists know black holes exist?
2. What is a white dwarf?
3. What happens when a star collapses?
4. What two forces keep the size of a star constant?
5. Where is the event horizon located?
6. Where is the singularity located?

Answer Key, Part A

1. a 2. b 3. a 4. c 5. b 6. a

Answer Key, Part B

Sample Answers:

1. Travel through a wormhole is unlikely because it is not stable and would collapse if you entered. Also, some think that the black hole and white hole must be identical. Moreover, the radiation inside would probably kill you.
2.

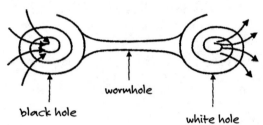

black hole   wormhole   white hole

Unit 7 Animal Talk

Quiz Audioscript, Part A

1. What type of communication involves communicating emotion?
2. What does a vervet monkey do when it hears an eagle alarm call?
3. According to the speaker, what kinds of animals use food calls?
4. What is an example of deceptive behavior in chickens?
5. What can humans do that animals cannot do?
6. What can some songbirds do?

Answer Key, Part A

1. b 2. b 3. a 4. b 5. c 6. c

Answer Key, Part B

Sample Answers:

1. A referent is the object, person, or idea that a signaler encodes and a receiver decodes. An example of an animal using a referent is a monkey giving a warning call to other monkeys.
2. It appears that animals intend to communicate. For example, wild birds often communicate about the presence of food when members of their own species are present. However, they may be quiet when no other birds are present.

Unit 8 Gender Differences in Language

Quiz Audioscript, Part A

1. What rose 33 percent between the 1920s and the 1990s?
2. What can people generally guess from transcribed speech?
3. What percentage of our work hours do we spend communicating?
4. What percentage of gender differences in communication styles is caused by the environment?
5. What phrase describes women's communication style?
6. According to the speaker, what two topics have men tended to discuss?

Answer Key, Part A

1. a   2. a   3. c   4. c   5. b   6. b

Answer Key, Part B

Sample Answers:

1. Both genetic and environmental factors cause gender differences. Genetic factors include differences in men and women's brain structures and hormone production. Environmental factors include how boys and girls are socialized.
2. Boys tend to practice more work-related skills, such as building a truck. These activities are more competition-oriented. In contrast, girls tend to practice more intimacy-related skills, such as dressing baby dolls and playing house. These activities are more collaboration-oriented.

Unit 9 Fashion and Status

Quiz Audioscript, Part A

1. Where did the Sumptuary laws originate?
2. What clothing features indicated social status in ancient Rome?
3. What is an example of conspicuous wealth?
4. What is an example of conspicuous multiplication?
5. Why is polyester no longer fashionable?
6. Why are designer clothes so expensive?

Answer Key, Part A

1. b   2. b   3. c   4. a   5. c   6. b

Answer Key, Part B

Sample Answers:

1. Conspicuous division is wearing different clothes for different activities. For example, today people wear different kinds of clothing when they golf, jog, and do aerobics.
2. Conspicuous outrage is wearing clothes that shock people because they do not conform. An example is wearing a torn T-shirt with bad language printed on it.

Unit 10 The Making of Genius

Quiz Audioscript, Part A

1. What innate ability may contribute to skill development?
2. What do the continued improvements in Olympic records show?
3. What types of memory are well developed in world chess masters?
4. What happens to young children when parents don't support their interests?
5. How much practice is needed to become an exceptional performer?
6. Why is it hard to measure innate talent?

Answer Key, Part A

1. c   2. a   3. b   4. c   5. b   6. c

Answer Key, Part B

Sample Answers:

1. Children need financial and emotional support in order to master a skill. For example, their parents may buy equipment, pay for lessons, and encourage them to practice long hours. Also, their teachers may also encourage them to work hard.
2. Working memory capacity and personality factors contribute to skill development. Working memory capacity, the ability to remember information, helps children to analyze and solve problems. Personality factors such as persistence enable children to practice intensely for a long time.

Unit 11 The New Global Superculture

Quiz Audioscript, Part A

1. According to the speaker, what has most influenced the globalization of ideas?
2. According to the speaker, what has most influenced the globalization of fads?
3. Why do many movies and TV shows have universal appeal?
4. According to the speaker, what is the best way of measuring cultural diversity?

5. According to the speaker, how do immigrants contribute to their new cultures?
6. According to the speaker, what are two negative effects of technology?

Answer Key, Part A

1. c   2. a   3. c   4. c   5. a   6. a

Answer Key, Part B

Sample Answers:

1. Cheap air travel has allowed people to interact with other cultures. This has led to the global spread of fads and technology. The communications industries, in the form of movies, soap operas, and advertising, have enabled viewers to see other ways of life and helped spread fads.
2. One advantage of a global superculture is that it shows that everybody basically wants the same things. This promotes a sense of unity. By breaking down prejudice and racial divisions, the global superculture can make the world a fairer place.

Unit 12 Computer Security

Quiz Audioscript, Part A

1. What percentage of companies have experienced computer fraud?
2. Who is the typical hacker?
3. How do hackers shut down computer systems?
4. What do hackers typically steal from individual computer users?
5. What can be used to trace hackers?
6. What stops information from entering a company's intranet?

Answer Key, Part A

1. a   2. a   3. c   4. a   5. c   6. a

Answer Key, Part B

Sample Answers:

1. People engage in computer crime for several reasons. First, they may want to steal and sell sensitive information, such as sensitive business information. Second, they may want to steal money. Third, they may enjoy the challenge.
2. In a typical hacking scenario, a hacker sends a virus to other computer users via the Internet. The virus enters the user's computer operating system and replaces good files with copies of itself. Then it sends itself to other users through the computer user's e-mail address book.

STUDENT BOOK ANSWER KEYS

Unit 1 Slang: Talking *Cool*

Vocabulary Preview, Part A, pages 2–3

1. b   2. a   3. c   4. c   5. a   6. b
7. a   8. b   9. a   10. a   11. c   12. b

Listening for Main Ideas, Part B, page 5

1. a   2. b   3. a, c   4. b   5. a   6. c

Listening for Details, Part B, pages 5–6

(Note: Corrected statements may vary.)

1. T

2. F (Young men and women use ~~different~~ *the same* slang expressions.)

3. T

4. F (Slang is ~~rarely~~ *often* humorous.)

5. T

6. T

7. T

8. F (Students use ~~more~~ *less* slang than colloquial vocabulary.)

Using Your Notes, Part A, pages 6–7

Sample Notes:

3 Types of Slang Words
  Type 1: Currently popular slang
    Examples: dope
            chill out
            the bomb
  —often terms of approval/disapproval
  —some "work hard"—used often with
    many meanings
  Type 2: Slang that stays from decade to decade
    Examples: cool
            nerd
            the man
  Type 3: Words that disappear
    Examples: gimme five
            how's it hanging
            core
  —often associated with personalities
    that come and go

Unit 2 Murphy's Law

Vocabulary Preview, Part A, page 9

Possible Answers:

1. expect; know what will happen
2. think something is true; understand that

3. circular movement; turning around 360 degrees
4. likely to happen; chance; possibility
5. without a pattern or plan
6. very bad event
7. meet; experience
8. happening in many places or to many people
9. something with a beginning, middle, and end; events experienced by living things
10. belief; idea
11. simple; basic
12. piece of equipment; machine

Listening for Main Ideas, Part B, page 12

1. a   2. b   3. c   4. c   5. b

Listening for Details, Part B, pages 12–13

1. F (There is ~~a 50~~ *an almost 100* percent chance that toast will land buttered-side up.)

2. F (The rate of spin of toast allows it to make ~~one~~ *half of a* revolution (360° turn) before it hits the ground.)

3. T

4. T

5. F (Scientists believe that single-event probabilities ~~cannot~~ *can* be calculated mathematically.)

6. T

7. T

Unit 3 Types of Memory

Vocabulary Preview, Part A, page 17

1. k   2. j   3. f   4. a   5. c   6. e
7. b   8. d   9. g   10. i   11. l   12. h

Listening for Main Ideas, Part B, page 20

Sample Outline:

I. Three types of memory
  A. Sensory memory
  B. Working memory
  C. Long-term memory
II. Three ways of measuring memory
  A. Recall
  B. Recognition
  C. Relearning

Listening for Details, Part B, page 20

1. short-term
2. under a half second
3. Working
4. doing mathematics
5. main ideas
6. one minute
7. recall
8. recognition
9. relearning

Unit 4 Actions Speak Louder than Words

Vocabulary Preview, Part A, page 24

Possible Answers:

1. something that interferes with someone's privacy
2. to communicate information
3. majority; greater part
4. caused; affected
5. exciting; active
6. to notice a difference
7. clearer explanation
8. strong feeling; passion
9. necessary; important
10. very small
11. opinion; feeling
12. guess

Listening for Main Ideas, Part B, pages 26–27

Sample Outline:

I. Birdwhistle—nonverbal communication (nvc)
   A. Studied—nvc in 1950s
   B. Believed—meaning of nvc depends on context
II. Porter—4 types nvc
   A. Physical = body language = kinesics
      1. Static
         a. Distance
         b. Orientation
         c. Posture
         d. Physical contact
      2. Dynamic
         a. Facial expressions
         b. Gestures
         c. Eye contact
         d. Body movement
   B. Aesthetic
   C. Signs
   D. Symbolic
III. V. com vs. nvc
   A. Emot. Same—diff. count.
   B. Know little about grammar of nvc

C. No dictionaries for nvc
D. Can't ask for clarification with nvc
E. Hard to hide true feelings with nvc

Listening for Details, Part B, pages 27–28

(Note: Corrected statements may vary.)

1. T
2. F (Ten percent to 30 percent of our communication is *verbal* ~~nonverbal~~.)
3. F (Raymond Birdwhistle began studying nonverbal communication in the ~~1960s~~ *1950s*.)
4. F (Signal flags and sirens are examples of ~~symbolic~~ *signs* ~~nonverbal communication.~~)
5. T
6. T
7. F (Facial expressions such as smiles have the same *do not* ^ meaning in each situation.)
8. F (Scientists understand ~~more~~ *less* about hand movements than any other gestures.)
9. T

Unit 5 Marriage: Traditions and Trends

Vocabulary Preview, Part A, pages 32–33

1. b   2. c   3. a   4. b   5. c   6. a
7. a   8. c   9. c   10. a   11. b   12. a

Listening for Main Ideas, Part B, pages 35–36

1. c   2. a   3. a   4. a   5. b   6. a

Listening for Details, Part B, page 36

1. The institution of marriage is ~~several million~~ *thousands of* years old.
2. The institution of marriage is *not* ^ disappearing.
3. Adoption is an example of ~~gender bias~~ *social parenthood*.
4. Endogamy is ~~not~~ *very* important in most societies.
5. The speaker has a brother whose marriage is an example of ~~endogamy~~ *exogamy*.

6. Traditionally, marriage was ~~a private decision between~~ *the decision of the whole family or tribe* ~~two people.~~

7. Marrying for love was ~~common~~ *very uncommon* in ancient societies.

8. Extended families are ~~replacing~~ *being replaced by* nuclear families in many countries.

Unit 6 Black Holes, White Holes, and Wormholes

Vocabulary Preview, Part A, page 40

Possible Answers:

1. to become smaller
2. unchanging
3. turns around
4. subject to disagreement; arguable
5. scientifically proven
6. don't believe
7. the same
8. by using
9. stopped
10. to fall down
11. ideas
12. safe; difficult to harm

Listening for Main Ideas, Part B, page 42

1. **a.** gravitational force **b.** event horizon **c.** singularity
2. **a.** black hole **b.** wormhole **c.** white hole

Listening for Details, Part B, page 43

(Note: Corrected statements may vary.)

1. F (The term "black hole" describes the final stage in the life of a ~~small~~ *very large* star.)

2. T
3. T

4. F (The ~~smaller~~ *larger* the size of a collapsing star, the greater its gravitational pull.)

5. F (The singularity of a black hole is very dense and ~~lightweight~~ *heavy*.)

6. F (Matter pours ~~into~~ *out of* a white hole.)

7. T

8. F (In theory, time travel through ~~non-rotating~~ *rotating* black holes is possible.)

9. F (There is mathematical proof that wormholes *could* exist.)

10. F (Wormholes are *not* stable.)

Unit 7 Animal Talk

Vocabulary Preview, Part A, pages 47–48

1. c   2. c   3. a   4. b   5. c   6. b
7. b   8. c   9. c   10. b   11. a   12. b

Listening for Main Ideas, Part B, page 50

1. a   2. c   3. b   4. a   5. a

Listening for Details, Part B, page 51

Possible Answers:

1. Each species has its own way of communicating, and some are different from what humans use.
2. Forms of animal communication include electrical currents, vibrations, ultrasonic signals, and odors.
3. Vervet monkeys seem to have a general alarm call and more specific calls for leopards, eagles, and snakes.
4. Monkeys and birds use food calls.
5. Scientists think that chickens are not intelligent enough to consciously lie.
6. The species and gender of other birds seem to affect whether birds make food calls.
7. Bird songs are created by manipulating different notes in different patterns.
8. Birds may use songs to advertise themselves, attract a mate, or express an emotion.

Unit 8 Gender Differences in Language

Vocabulary Preview, Part A, page 54

Possible Answers:

1. an incorrect idea that many people have of what a particular type of person is like
2. separation of different groups of people
3. current; modern
4. opinion; feeling
5. very important; necessary
6. strengthened; supported
7. to show
8. to start
9. inherited; present at birth
10. powerful
11. focused on
12. to participate in

Listening for Main Ideas, Part B, pages 57–58

1. c **2.** b **3.** b **4.** b **5.** b **6.** c

Listening for Details, Part B, pages 58–59

(Note: Corrected statements may vary.)

1. T

2. F (We spend ~~60~~ 70 percent of our working hours communicating.)

3. F (Genetic factors ~~do not~~ influence male and female communication styles.) [a lot ^]

4. T

5. F (Having discussions about relationships helps develop a ~~competition~~-oriented communication style.) [collaboration]

6. T

7. T

8. F (Male and female communication styles are the same in all cultures.) [not ^]

Unit 9 Fashion and Status

Vocabulary Preview, Part A, page 62

1. b **2.** h **3.** a **4.** k **5.** e **6.** d
7. i **8.** c **9.** g **10.** j **11.** l **12.** f

Listening for Main Ideas, Part B, page 65

Sample outline:

I. Sumptuary Laws
   Definition: Laws controlling type, color, and number of garments
II. Conspicuous Consumption—8 types
   A. Conspicuous addition
      Definition: Wearing more clothes than other people
   B. Conspicuous division
      Definition: Wearing a lot of clothes consecutively
   C. Conspicuous multiplication
      Definition: Owning and displaying many similar garments
   D. Conspicuous materials
      Definition: Wearing expensive materials
   E. Conspicuous wealth
      Definition: Displaying expensive items, usually jewelry
   F. Conspicuous labeling
      Definition: Using easily seen labels to show expensive brands
   G. Conspicuous outrage
      Definition: Dressing to shock people
   H. Associative consumption
      Definition: Wearing clothes that are associated with high-status people

Listening for Details, Part B, page 66

Possible Answers:

1. Sumptuary laws became difficult to enforce because the barriers between social classes became weaker.
2. An example of conspicuous addition at the beach is having a shirt, hat, and bag that match your swimsuit.
3. An example of conspicuous multiplication among very wealthy men is wearing a new shirt every day.
4. Satin and velvet were prestigious because they were hand-made and required much time and labor to produce.
5. Silk, leather, and wool are prestigious today because they're natural and scarcer.
6. Some designer garments have labels on the outside so that people can see they are expensive.
7. Clothes with designer labels are expensive because of the cost of advertising them.
8. An example of conspicuous outrage is wearing a faded T-shirt with bad language printed on it.

Unit 10 The Making of Genius

Vocabulary Preview, Part A, pages 70–71

1. a **2.** b **3.** c **4.** a **5.** b **6.** a
7. c **8.** c **9.** a **10.** a **11.** b **12.** a

Listening for Main Ideas, Part B, pages 73–74

1. a **2.** a **3.** c **4.** c **5.** b **6.** c

Listening for Details, Part B, page 74

(Note: Corrected statements may vary.)

1. F (Some people thought ~~Wolfgang Amadeus Mozart~~ had magical powers.) [Niccolò Paganini]

2. F (Expert chess players have better ~~general~~ memory skills than most people.) [specialized]

3. T

4. T

5. F (Expert musicians ~~often~~ show signs of greatness by the age of five.) [do not]

6. **An unknown**
   F (~~About 15~~ percent of our personality characteristics and intelligence are genetically determined.)
7. T
8. T

Using Your Notes, Part A, page 75

Correct order of steps: 5, 6, 2, 1, 7, 3, 4

Unit 11 The New Global Superculture

Vocabulary Preview, Part A, page 79

1. a 2. i 3. j 4. h 5. l 6. f
7. d 8. k 9. g 10. e 11. c 12. b

Listening for Main Ideas, Part B, pages 82–83

1. a 2. c 3. a 4. a 5. c

Listening for Details, Part B, page 83

Possible Answers:

1. Language and the rate at which languages are dying
2. Technological and social
3. Electronic technology, clothing, perfume, and fast foods
4. They are based on universal human problems.
5. It has helped spread fads globally.
6. They have increased the number of people who immigrate to other countries.
7. It has increased cross-cultural contact and the spread of ideas.
8. The Ainu are from Japan, the Chipaya are from Bolivia, and the Penan are from Malaysia.

Unit 12 Computer Security

Vocabulary Preview, Part A, pages 88–89

1. a 2. c 3. b 4. b 5. c 6. b
7. b 8. a 9. c 10. a 11. b 12. a

Listening for Main Ideas, Part B, page 92

Sample Outline:

I. Reasons for computer crime
   A. Stealing and selling information (financial gain)
   B. Stealing money (financial gain)
   C. Exciting challenge
II. Effects of computer crime
   A. On companies and/or governments
      1. Lost work hours, shut down computers
   B. On individuals
      1. Inconvenience
      2. Financial loss
III. Possible solutions
   A. Tougher punishment for criminals
   B. Firewalls
   C. Difficult passwords
   D. Access-control software
   E. Encryption software
   F. Audit trails

Listening for Details, Part B, pages 92–93

(Note: Corrected statements may vary.)

1. **40**
   F (About ~~50~~ percent of companies that are online have experienced computer crime.)
2. T
3. T
4. F (Computer viruses have ~~not~~ affected government computer systems.)
5. F (The courts' attitude toward computer crime has **gotten much tougher** ~~changed little~~ in recent years.)
6. T
7. F (A word chosen from a large dictionary is an **not** ^ effective password.)
8. T
9. T
10. T

Unit 1 Slang: Talking *Cool*

TEACHER: OK, let's get started . . . Today we're going to be looking at a really interesting *phenomenon*, slang. We'll be looking at where slang comes from, who uses it and why. We all use it more often than you might think—every day of our lives, in fact. And we use it for a reason.

You know, most of us are fascinated with slang. We continually hear new words and phrases enter the language and replace old, and we see familiar words take on new meanings. We feel a need to keep in touch with these changes, to be aware of the latest street talk. Fact is, we love slang. But what is it exactly? What is slang? Anyone like to suggest a definition?

STUDENT 1: Isn't it basically kind of casual talk?

TEACHER: Can you say a bit more?

STUDENT 1: You know, the sort of words we use with friends . . . in relaxed situations.

TEACHER: Good. You're pretty much there with your idea of casual language. We can say that slang is language that's found only in the very informal speech of particular groups of people. It can help to identify the communities, the groups of people, who use it. And this brings me to the first important point of the lecture—why people use slang.

A lot of slang comes from not wanting to be understood by outsiders, people outside your circle. In other words, people *exploit* slang to give their group an identity, by making their language exclusive, or at least private. Through this private language, they can tease one another, enjoy shared experiences, and keep everyone else at a distance. All cultures contain groups or subcultures with different interests and *priorities*, and each group tries to establish a separate identity. They want people to know who they are, what they stand for—and slang helps to *construct* and cement that identity. We can say, then, that slang reflects the experiences, beliefs, and values of its speakers.

Now let's look more closely at this relationship between slang and community, slang and identity. A nice example of this is, uh, student language, sometimes called "youth-speak." Young people use a lot of slang, and many of the words they use are used by both sexes, often metaphorically rather than literally. That is to say, the conventional meaning of the words change. For example, words that have traditionally had strong negative literal meanings that are used as insults have taken on, uh, gentler, and in many cases even positive meanings in conversation. We'll look at some examples later.

Now, if you ask college students why they use slang, they'll tell you it's cool, and that's true in several different ways. First, it's cool because it's in style, in fashion. Using current slang shows that the speaker is in tune with the times . . . you know, that he or she knows what's in fashion and is part of that fashion.

Second, slang is cool in the sense of showing that the speaker is knowledgeable . . . the speaker is "in the know," the speaker knows when slang is acceptable. People don't use slang all the time, only in situations and with people who accept the use of slang—a point I'll return to later. Research tells us that although young people often deny that they use slang intentionally, in fact they clearly choose whether or not to use it depending on the situation they're in. As we've already said, slang's typically used in informal rather than formal settings, and this is certainly true among college students: They usually avoid using it in the classroom or a work environment, for example. Anyone like to suggest why?

STUDENT 1: People won't understand them.

STUDENT 2: Yeah, so it's like a waste of time.

TEACHER: Well, that may be true, but it's not the main reason. They *don't* use it simply because it could make them look bad. And everyone hates looking bad, right?

So, to review, we've said that students use slang only in certain situations. But they also only use it with certain people, usually friends. When they use slang, they are showing that they share social and emotional experiences—so slang reinforces their relationships. But . . . it also gives special meaning to what they say. For instance, to say "That party was the bomb" is more than merely saying it was a very good party. It shares an emotional experience that might otherwise take several sentences to explain. In other words, it's a kind of . . . shorthand.

The third and final way slang's cool is that it's fun; it's very creative in the same way that poetry is, and it's often humorous. In other words, it's a form of play, a way of entertaining.

So . . . uh, let me repeat: I've said that slang's cool for three reasons: One, it shows the user's fashionable and in tune with the times; two, it's a way of reinforcing relationships and communicating efficiently; and three, it's fun and entertaining. Got that?

All right then, let's now take a look at different kinds of slang, in particular three types of slang words: those that are currently most used, those that linger year after year, and those that have become unfashionable.

So . . . now what *is* the most used slang? Well, research tells us that over the past few years, in the number one position is "dope," which basically means very good, great, excellent, attractive, or nice. So somebody might say, for example, that his friend's new motorbike is really dope; in other words, it's very good. Other words that feature in the top twenty include "chill out" (to calm down or relax), "the bomb" (meaning the best or most excellent), "whack" (which means bad, unfair, crazy, or foolish), and "dude" (meaning person—usually a man, actually). Any other examples? Yes?

STUDENT 1: Hella.

TEACHER: Meaning?

STUDENT 1: Very, a lot.

TEACHER: OK, yep. Luis?

STUDENT 3: "Kick it," which means, like, to hang out, uh, relax, you know, sit around doing nothing.

TEACHER: Right. And it's interesting, isn't it, how most slang terms indicate approval or disapproval; they show what we feel positive or negative about. So, like "dope" and "the bomb," we have "sweet," "phat"—spelled P-H-A-T, not F-A-T-"cool," and "tight"—all meaning good, excellent, nice, or attractive.

And then you have words like "bad" which really mean good; so "That new CD is bad" actually means it's good! So you see, slang does strange things with language. Like I said earlier, it's certainly creative. As a matter of fact, some slang words have many different meanings, sometimes as many as nine or ten. For instance, the word "trip" or "tripping" has various meanings, but they all reflect the idea of unusual, strange, or extreme. When a word's used a lot or has a number of different meanings like this, we sometimes say it "*works* hard." The word "trip," then, is a word that works hard.

Uh . . . now, the second type of slang consists of words that linger from *decade* to decade and never seem to go out of fashion—and these words also work hard, that is, they have a lot of meanings. A great example is the word *cool*— forever popular, it seems! Other terms in this category are "nerd," "cheesy," "chick," "the man," "toasted," "wasted," "what's up," "blow away," and "gross." And once again, most of these show approval or disapproval.

And . . . now, finally, there are slang terms that come and go; they disappear almost as quickly as they appear. Examples include "gimme five," "how's it hanging," and "core." Words like these often disappear because they're closely *associated with* famous personalities who similarly come and go—they're popular, in the spotlight for a while, and then seem almost to disappear. And when they disappear, the slang associated with them tends to disappear as well.

Now, today, public tolerance of slang is at an all-time high—just look at how widely it's used in newspapers. But how do college teachers and academics view slang? Well, some *persist with* the idea that its use will degrade . . . uh, you might even say "pollute" academic discourse. However, among themselves students *tolerate* words their teachers might consider *taboo*. Students are actually very good at code-switching; that is, they're very good at using different styles or codes of communication in different situations. Do you agree? Do you use slang in your essays or when you speak with a teacher?

STUDENT 3: Personally I never use slang in essays. It just doesn't feel right. It's true, you know, most students know when to use slang, and when not to.

STUDENT 2: I agree. I sometimes use it with teachers, though; it just depends on who the teacher is.

TEACHER: Why, I imagine most people do the same. Here's something you may find surprising: A recent study on student conversation suggests that students don't in fact use slang that often but instead they choose more ordinary *colloquial* vocabulary.

OK, to finish up, now let me say something about the history of slang. Many years ago, slang was closely associated with underground, criminal organizations, groups that *deviate* from *mainstream* society . . . uh . . . with notions of outcasts and socially unacceptable behaviors. A look back in time shows, for example, that in the seventeenth century more than twenty words were used to refer to vagrants, that is, to someone who has no home or job. Today, of course, these associations are much weaker and slang's used much more widely. As underground culture has become more mainstream, there's not the same need for the kind of secret code that slang offered. Today, most of us use slang and aren't ashamed of using it. It may still have negative connotations, but like it or not it's here to stay, and increasingly it's become the subject of serious academic study. And why not? As I've tried to show, it's a fascinating social as well as linguistic phenomenon. So, any questions? . . .

Unit 2 Murphy's Law

TEACHER: Good afternoon, everyone. More than 200 years ago, the Scottish poet Robert Burns said that "the best laid plans of mice and men often go awry." I'm sure we all have firsthand experience with what Burns means; no matter how carefully we plan a project and no matter how carefully we try to, uh, *anticipate* problems, we're likely to, uh *encounter* something unexpected and unwelcome that will throw our plan off course.

Well, class today we'll be looking at how plans can go right or wrong . . . and, uh, how we can make sense of this. Are you all familiar with Murphy's Law? Well, according to Murphy's Law, anything that can go wrong will go wrong. So we'll be looking at everyday examples of Murphy's Law—uh, things like why toast falls buttered-side down, why it always seems like we choose slow lines at the supermarket, and why it is so difficult to win when we gamble.

As you may know, we now have many different versions of Murphy's Law, and today I'd like to look at the science behind three of them. I'll try to show you that some things which have happened to you, and which you may have thought were simply bad luck, had nothing to do with luck at all. What I'm saying is that there are some very good scientific reasons for many of the things that happen to us, and we're not victims of bad luck as often as we might think. When we consider some basic science and *probability theory*, we can more clearly understand why some "bad" things happen the way they do.

All right. Let's begin with a very commonplace situation. Let's say you've just gotten up. You're still sleepy, and you make your way to the breakfast table. In your half-awake state, you accidentally hit your piece of toast, which has butter on one side. The toast begins to fall to the floor. Now what are the chances that you'll be lucky and the toast will land buttered-side up? Well, the toast has only two sides, so most people think that the answer is fifty–fifty. Fifty percent. Right? Do you think that there's a 50 percent chance that the toast will land with the buttered-side up?

STUDENT 1: Well, this sounds like a trick question, but, uh, yeah. Logically, 50 percent sounds about right.

TEACHER: Yes, 50 percent does *seem* right, but, in this case, Murphy's Law of Falling Toast says: "Toast which falls from a table will land buttered-side down." Actually, the probability of this happening is extremely high. It's close to 100 percent. Now, here's why. When something like a piece of toast falls from a table, its behavior is not *random*. The rate of spin is controlled by the laws of physics. This is the problem. The rate of spin, that is, how fast the toast spins, is too low for the toast to make a complete *revolution*. It's too slow to turn completely around and hit the floor buttered-side up. The rate of spin is determined by the force of gravity. So in a very real sense, the laws of physics, and specifically the rate of spin, make sure that our toast lands buttered-side down almost all the time. So the point is that simple probabilities—for example, the probability that toast has a fifty–fifty chance of landing buttered-side up—can be greatly affected by other more *fundamental* factors, such as the laws of physics. So, in this case, we believe that we have bad luck because we don't understand that the natural laws of physics are in effect. The toast *should* land buttered-side down. OK? Let's look at the next point.

Now we come to one of my most frustrating situations in life—the supermarket line. In this case, Murphy's Law of Supermarket Lines says: "The line next to you will move faster than yours." Now everybody wants to get into the fastest line when they go to the supermarket, right? OK, so let's say that you're at your local supermarket and there are five lines, but each of the five lines looks pretty much equal in length. Now, of course, you want to try to anticipate which one of the five lines will move the fastest. Well, this is where simple probability theory enters the picture. The chances that you have chosen the fastest of the five lines is one divided by the number of lines, which is five in this case. So mathematically, the formula is one divided by N where N is the total number of lines. So in this example, one divided by five gives us what?

STUDENT 2: One divided by five is one-fifth or . . . uh . . . 20 percent.

TEACHER: Right. Twenty percent. There's only a 20 percent chance that we have chosen the fastest of the five lines. Now even if we reduce that to three lines, our line and the lines on each side of us, the chances we've chosen the fastest line are still only what?

STUDENT 2: Uh, 33 percent. One out of three.

TEACHER: Sure. One divided by three is 33 percent, so it's not just your imagination that one line near you almost always moves faster than yours. Simple probability theory shows that the odds are against you. If there are very many lines, the chances that you'll choose the fastest one is quite low. So, you see, it has little to do with luck, but we *perceive* that it does.

All right. Now let's look at a final situation that shows how we commonly misunderstand the laws of probability. We've come to Murphy's Law of Gambling that says simply: "You will lose." Now in the case of the supermarket lines that we've just talked about, probability theory applied very nicely. And actually, as we go through life, most things are fairly predictable because they follow the basic laws of probability. Weather is an example. Let's say that it's been raining for a week, and a friend says to you "I think it's going to be sunny tomorrow." Is that an unreasonable statement? Well, no. Clouds move, and they are of limited size, so if it's been raining for a week, it's likely that the rain and clouds will end soon. In other words, the next sunny day is more likely to occur after the seventh day of rain than after the first, because the storm front has what is called a *life history*. Now this is important, so let me explain that term. Events with a life history have changing probabilities of certain events occurring over time. For instance, uh, if you plant flower seeds, you can predict with reasonable accuracy when the plants will come up, when they will bloom, and how long they will bloom. For instance, with some types of flowers, there's a 90 percent chance that they will come up fifteen to twenty days after the seeds have been planted. In short, the growth of a flower follows a clear predictable pattern, and we call this pattern a life history. But this is the trick with many gambling games. The casino owners want us to believe that dice also have a life history and that we can therefore estimate the probability of events related to the dice. However, gambling *devices* like dice are different because they don't have life histories. Now . . . what do you think that means?

STUDENT 1: There aren't any reliable patterns? Um, just because I rolled a seven last time doesn't tell me anything about the next roll.

TEACHER: Right. You can't look at the past rolls of the dice and predict what the next roll will be. Now many people, especially gamblers, think that they can, but this is what's called the gambler's fallacy. The gambler's fallacy is expecting to roll a seven with a pair of dice because a seven hasn't come up recently. So, in other words, there's a *widespread* belief among gamblers that dice have a life history. In the real world, that's not a bad way to reason, but in a casino, it's the path to financial loss. Dice have no memory, no life history. Now you *can* predict that if you roll one dice many, many times, the number five will come up about 16 percent of the time. That's one divided by six. But that's not what we're concerned with here. We're concerned with the next roll of the dice. As a result, the element of arbitrariness or randomness makes prediction of the next roll impossible. Statisticians who work with probability theory call the roll of a pair of dice a single-event probability, and many of these same statisticians believe that the probability of a single event can't even be computed mathematically. So, the same probability theory that works well with supermarket lines won't help you win a million dollars in a dice game in Las Vegas. It could, in fact, lead to a *catastrophe*!

So, to sum up, we have looked at three cases involving Murphy's Law and our perception of "bad luck." The first case was the toast, right? Our toast lands buttered-side down far more often than we would predict because the basic laws of physics have a strong effect on normal probabilities. The second case was the supermarket line, remember? Another line moves faster than ours because the laws of probability are behaving normally, even though we might perceive them as behaving unfairly. And the third case was the dice game. People lose at gambling games like dice because the laws of "life history probability" simply don't apply in those situations, even though gamblers think they do.

So, as you can see, in some cases, Murphy's Law is not just some form of bad luck. There are some very real, scientific explanations for these events. OK, that's about it for today. For next class I'd like you to take a look at Chapter 7 and be ready to talk about the discussion questions on page 255. See you then.

Unit 3 Types of Memory

TEACHER: Good morning everyone. Um . . . today, I have the pleasure of introducing you to the basics of what I think is one of the most fascinating topics in the field of psychology—memory. What is memory? How does memory work? The research in this field is fascinating and dates back to the late 1800s, so it's been going on for more than a century. I'll begin today by saying a few things about three types of memory that we all have, and then we'll look at how memory is measured.

All right. First of all, let's begin by looking at types of memory. One of the most common ways to classify memory is based on time . . . based on time and *duration* of use. So typically, memory is divided into three types: sensory memory, working memory (which is also referred to as short-term memory), and long-term memory. Again, that's sensory memory, working memory, and long-term memory.

Let's talk about sensory memory for a minute. Sensory memory holds information for only an instant, say, less than half a second. This is just long enough to register an impression on one or more of our five senses—sight, hearing, touch, smell, or taste. Let me give you an example of a *phenomenon* concerning *visual* sensory memory that I'm sure you've all experienced. Imagine that you're holding up a flashlight on a dark night. You start to move it in circles slowly, watching it carefully the whole time. Pretty soon you aren't just seeing the flashlight . . . you can see a full circle of light! Of course, it's actually just one point of light being moved around, but your memory of the visual sensation of the light fills in the rest of the circle. That's one example of sensory memory. So remember, you can hold something in your sensory memory for just a fraction of a second, up to around half a second, then it *fades* away.

Now if you want to keep the information for longer than a second, you have to put it into your working memory. Working memory, the second type of memory, allows us to hold on to things for as long as we think about them, that is, as long as we're paying attention to them. It's something like a kind of *temporary* storage place. Let me give you a simple math problem. Are you ready? Here goes . . . 18 plus 44 plus 9 plus 19. . . I'll say that one more time. OK? 18 plus 44 plus 9 plus 19. . . . All right? . . . Do you all have the answer? Maya?

STUDENT 1: Uh, I think it's 90. Yeah, 90.

TEACHER: Let's see . . . 18 plus 44 is 62 . . . plus 9 is 71 . . . plus 19 is 90. Ninety is the answer. Now, to figure out this problem, you had to use your working memory. As you did the problem, you had to continue holding the numbers in your memory until you got the final answer. If you stopped concentrating on the numbers, that is, you stopped saying them to yourself, or stopped visualizing them, you would have forgotten them and then you wouldn't have been able to solve the problem. Do you see how that works?

Here's one more example of working memory involving reading. Look at the sentence: "Honey is the only natural food that is made without destroying any kind of life." It's written down in your textbook. Why, you may wonder, do we need working memory to understand such a simple sentence? Well, the answer is because working memory holds the first part of the sentence, "Honey is the only natural food . . ." while our eyes move on to the last part, that is, "made without destroying any kind of life." Without our working memory, we would forget the first part of the sentence before we got to the end. So reading even short or simple passages would be impossible without our working memory.

OK, I think you can see how important working memory is, but our working memory is very limited, and it can only hold information temporarily. It usually lasts only one and one half to two seconds and then it begins to fade. So if working memory were all we had, we would be very limited. Essentially, working memory mediates between how we experience the environment and our long-term memory. This brings us to the third type of memory that we'll talk about today, long-term memory.

Now, long-term memory is involved with information that's stored for considerable lengths of time. For example, do you remember the name of your best friend when you were ten years old? I bet you do, because this information is certainly in your long-term memory. Actually, memory that's tested after about one minute behaves in a very similar way to memory tested after a day, a week, or even years, so many scientists believe that any memories more than one minute old are part of our long-term memory. Interestingly, these memories seem to change over time in the sense that we tend to add information to them. In a sense, our memories become *somewhat distorted.* The reason behind these changes is that our memory is designed to keep or preserve meaning, not to keep impressions or images, but to keep meaning. For example, try to remember a conversation you had yesterday with a friend. Now if you're like most people, you can't remember the exact words that you or your friend said, but you can remember the ideas that you discussed. Your memories of the points that were most important to you will be the clearest. So the *essential* feature of long-term memory is that it specializes in holding meaning. OK, are there any questions about that? Yes?

STUDENT 1: Yeah. Can you explain why we don't remember all of the details of our past conversations?

TEACHER: So the question is, "Why do we forget?" Well, most experts believe that if we remembered all of the details of our past experiences, our memory system would be filled with a lot of trivial information, a lot of trivial and generally useless information. Secondly, it is *conceivable* that we would find it extremely difficult to sift through such a . . . a mass of *detailed* information and find the really important information that we need. Um . . . in other words, memory searches would proceed a lot more slowly.

STUDENT 1: OK, I see. Thank you.

TEACHER: OK, let's move on to ways of measuring memory. Just as we *distinguished* three types of memory, there are three main ways of measuring how much a person remembers. The first of these methods is called recall. You use recall many times every day. Here's what I mean. . . . Take out a sheet of paper. . . . OK, now look at the word list in your text: drum, band, studio, and so on. . . . Read it silently to yourself. . . . OK? . . . Have you looked at all of the words? . . . OK, you should be finished by now. Now, close your book. Write down the words you saw, as many as you can, on your paper. . . . Go ahead. . . . OK, that's a simple recall test. Now, most of you probably remembered most of the words, but not all of them. Our memories, of course, are not perfect, and of course forgetting is natural.

The second method of measuring memory is recognition. OK, for this you need another piece of paper, or just turn that one over. . . . All right. Number the page from one to eight. . . . Now look at the word list again. OK, now close your book. I'm going to say eight words. You have to write "yes" or "no"—"yes" if the word I say was on the list, "no" if the word I say was not on the list. Ready? Here I go. 1. studio. 2. guitar. 3. stage. 4. recorder. 5. wiring. 6. song 7. vocalist. 8. drum. . . . OK, everybody finished? The answers are 1. yes, 2. no, 3. yes, 4. no, 5. yes, 6. no, 7. yes, and 8. yes. . . . How did you do? Anyone get all eight correct? . . . Good! That's what we call a recognition test. In contrast to the recall test, recognition is more receptive and doesn't require you to produce anything. For this reason,

recognition is a lot easier for most of us than recall. In other words, asking yourself "Have I seen this before?" is easier than remembering everything you saw.

Now the third basic method used to measure memory is relearning. Let me give you an example of a relearning test. First, you try to memorize a list of words. Then you don't look at the list for a period of time, maybe a week. If you're like most people, you won't be able to remember all of the words. After a week, you then look at the list a second time and try to relearn it. As you would guess, most people relearn information somewhat faster than they learn it the first time. By measuring the time people need to relearn information, we can *calculate* how much information they have stored in their long-term memories the first time.

So, let's stop there for today. Uh . . . I hope that you'll put today's material in your long-term memory . . . or you're going to have a hard time with the test. See you next week.

Unit 4 Actions Speak Louder than Words

TEACHER: OK, class, OK . . . let's begin. What do we mean when we say that actions speak louder than words?

STUDENT 1: Uh . . . that means we believe people's actions more than we believe their words.

TEACHER: Yes, exactly right—and, uh, in a sense, actions are more important than words. That's because we usually judge speakers' intentions by the nonverbal signals they send us. And that's what our subject today's all about, nonverbal communication—how we communicate through our actions—facial expressions, eye contact, tone of voice, uh, body movement, and so on. And if any of you doubt the importance of these things, you might like to consider a couple of statistics I've got here in front of me. Some communication specialists *estimate* we spend about 75 percent of our waking hours communicating. And, more to the point, words account for only, mm, 10 to 30 percent of that communication—the *bulk's* nonverbal. That's food for thought, uh?

Now although people clearly understand its importance, nonverbal communication—I'll call it N.V.C. for short—is actually a rather recent field of study and owes a lot to an American anthropologist named Raymond Birdwhistle—spelled B-I-R-D-W-H-I-S-T-L-E. Easy name to remember, right? Birdwhistle began studying nonverbal communication in the 1950s and, um . . . one of his main ideas was that the meaning of nonverbal behavior depended on the context in which it was used. . . . Uh, it depends on the context. So, he looked at the whole context of nonverbal behavior—how and, uh, where certain types of nonverbal behavior appeared—and not just one particular behavior in isolation. Facial expressions, for example—frowns, smiles, raised eyebrows, and, uh, so on—we all use these to *convey* many different meanings. But those meanings are largely *determined* by the situations we're in and the relationships that we have with the people we're communicating with. So, the same expression can have different meanings, right? Take a smile, for example, what does it mean? . . . Uh, Mike?

STUDENT 2: Uh . . . uh, agreement, I guess. "I like you."

TEACHER: OK. Yes, it could mean "I like you," but it could also mean "I'm trying to make you feel comfortable," or maybe, uh, "I think you said something funny." Hmm? The point is, the situation or the relationship between the people involved gives a particular meaning to the smile. All right.

Now although today I want to focus on physical nonverbal communication—uh, often called body language or kinesics, that's K-I-N-E-S-I-C-S—you should know that there are other types of nonverbal communication. G. W. Porter, for example, divides nonverbal communication into four categories, which I'd like to look at just briefly. There's the Physical N.V.C. I just mentioned. That includes facial expressions, tone of voice, sense of touch and smell, and body movement. Secondly, there's Aesthetic N.V.C.— that's A-E-S-T-H-E-T-I-C, meaning related to beauty. And Aesthetic N.V.C. takes place through creative expressions, like playing instrumental music, dancing or painting, sculpting. And we certainly know that we can communicate with people through creative expressions like these.

Now, next is Signs, which is a mechanical type of communication. Now, it includes the use of things like signal flags used at airports, the twenty-one gun salute used in the military, and police sirens used on public streets. And last is Symbolic N.V.C., which uses religious, status, or ego-building symbols—you know, things like wearing crosses in the Christian religion or special pins to show membership in a particular club, like a fraternity. So, again, you've got physical, aesthetic, signs, and symbolic nonverbal communication. Got that?

But let's go back to Porter's first type, Physical N.V.C., or body language . . . . Um, it's divided into two main types— static features and *dynamic* features. Static features include distance, orientation, posture, and physical contact. Let's look at distance first. The distance a person stands from another often sends a nonverbal message. In some situations it's a sign of attraction; in others it's a reflection of social status; in others it shows the *intensity* of the exchange. Distance has to do with personal space and what an *invasion* of someone's personal space signifies, what it means. Britney?

STUDENT 1: Yes, what is personal space exactly? Could you explain it a bit more, please?

TEACHER: Ah, well, good question. Well, it's kind of like a bubble each of us places between ourself and others—an invisible border or limit. Now this affects how close we stand to others, where we sit in a room, at a meeting, and uh, so on—things which affect how comfortable we feel. Generally speaking, the higher your status, the more space you'll have and the easier it'll be to invade other people's space. Uh, I hope that's clearer.

Now, orientation's different from distance and has to do with the way we position ourselves in relation to others. For example, people cooperating are likely to sit side-by-side, while competitors are likely to sit face to face . . . right? And posture's different again; it concerns whether we're slouched

or we're standing or sitting straight. You know: Are our legs crossed, our arms folded? That sort of thing. These convey the level of formality or relaxation in the same situation.

Then comes physical contact, and here we're talking about touching, holding, hugging, and so on. These convey or show messages—particularly how intimate we feel—and their meaning can vary a lot between cultures. Hands touching in one culture may be an act of great intimacy, whereas in another . . . simply a sign of friendship. The fact is, though, that touching and physical intimacy can send a more direct yet subtle message than dozens of words. Be careful though: This kind of communication can easily invade someone's personal space, and that can . . . lead, uh . . . cause mistrust, lead to problems—and actually shut down the communication.

So those are Porter's static features. Let's now look at his dynamic features. These are basically things like facial expressions, gestures, eye contact, and uh, body movements. Facial expressions, then . . . these continually change during a conversation, and participants constantly watch and respond to each others' expressions. These expressions usually communicate the emotions and *attitude* of the speaker. Take eyes for example; they. . . . Well, let me ask you, what do *you* think they reveal? Yes?

STUDENT 2: Um . . . happiness and sadness?

TEACHER: Fear? Fright?

STUDENT 3: Friendliness.

TEACHER: Yes, some of these things are revealed in the eyes, happiness and sadness yes . . . also fright and surprise. Think about it. Think about how your eyes respond when you hear something surprising, or frightening, or sad, or cheerful. Now, the lower face—the mouth and jaw—also reveals happiness or surprise, especially the smile, as we've said. The upper face, eyebrows, and forehead can also reveal anger. In some communication studies, it's been estimated that facial expressions provide 55 percent of the meaning of a message; vocal cues, such as pitch and volume, provide 38 percent; and verbal cues only 7 percent. So, a person's expressions seem to be a better indicator of his meaning than words, which play a *minimal* part.

OK, now where are we? Oh. We're looking at Porter's dynamic features of communication. Next we come to gestures. You know, one of the most important parts of gesturing, hand movements, is one of those least understood by scientists. Most are not universal, and as we all know, the same gesture can have different meanings in different countries. Here in the U.S. we make a circle with our thumb and first finger and it means "OK." In Japan, however, it means "money," and in South America it has a sexual meaning. The story goes that former President Richard Nixon made a huge mistake on a trip to South America when he held up both hands using this "OK." gesture. Needless to say, the people in the audience were quite shocked! The fact is, we have to be very careful about what our bodies are saying . . . especially when in a different culture.

Now let's move on to eye contact. Eye contact is a very powerful form of nonverbal communication. One thing about eye contact that is generally agreed on is that someone with higher status usually maintains eye contact longer if he's talking to someone of lower status. In other words, he stares. Anything else you think a direct stare indicates?

STUDENT 1: Determination . . . uh . . . openness.

TEACHER: Exactly, and it creates a feeling of trust. And looking downward?

STUDENT 1: That shows dishonesty, guilt, . . . uh . . .

TEACHER: Yes, it does, but also modesty, in some cases. And eyes rolled upwards suggest tiredness. I don't see any of that right now, I'm glad to say!

And the last, the fourth item on Porter's list is body movement. You know, it's interesting that a lot of the work on nonverbal communication has been done for corporations. They want to improve their employees' performance. So for example, if you lean forward in an interview, this suggests you're energetic, somebody prepared to make major changes. If you hold yourself at your tallest, uh, this suggests you're probably a presenter, and good at selling yourself or the organization. And with side-to-side movements, if you take up a lot of space while talking by moving your arms a lot, you're seen as a good informer and listener, so you're desirable to the company. See?

So to finish up, I'm going to list five things that *differentiate* verbal and nonverbal communication. I'd like you to note them down. First, while spoken languages differ from country to country, emotions are communicated in much the same nonverbal way throughout the world. Second, although we know a lot about the grammar of spoken language, we still don't know very much about the "grammar" of N.V.C. Third, we don't have any dictionaries for N.V.C. If you go to a foreign country and somebody makes a hand gesture you don't understand, there's no dictionary to help you. And fourth, we can ask for repetition or *clarification* of what somebody has said, but it's practically impossible to ask, "Could you repeat that smile?" or "What does that facial expression mean?" We have to understand nonverbal communication the first time around. And finally, we can hide our true feelings with spoken language, but it's more difficult with N.V.C. We can't just stop ourselves from turning red, or slow down our heartbeat, right? So whether we like it or not, body language can't lie—although I'll bet there are times we all wish it could.

So in conclusion then, nonverbal communication is an *integral* part of communication. OK, now let's quickly get into groups and talk about some of the differences I've just mentioned. This is what I want you to do. Just pull your chairs around. . . .

Unit 5 Marriage: Traditions and Trends

TEACHER: Good afternoon, class. Today I'd like to talk about a subject which is probably going to be very important in your future, for many of you at least—marriage. Marriage, as you probably know, has been with the human race for thousands of years. And, although some would say that the institution of marriage has come under attack in recent decades, marriage isn't going to disappear anytime soon. We're going to start today by looking at some definitions of marriage. Then, we'll consider the selection of a marriage partner, a critical decision that—you will see—has been handled very differently by different cultures. We'll see that how societies handle this question has changed in recent decades, and this change is having a strong impact on marriage in today's world.

OK. So what is marriage? This may seem like a simple question, but not every society answers it in the same way. Generally, we can describe marriage as a more or less durable union between one or more men and one or more women that is sanctioned by society. I know that's long, so let me repeat it. Marriage is a more or less durable union . . . between one or more men . . . and one or more women . . . that is sanctioned by, that is accepted by, society. All right? Now the words "sanctioned by society" are an important part of this definition because social approval is what distinguishes marriage from other relationships between adults. A second important point is that the *obligations* between partners—or the responsibilities that the partners have toward each other—are specified in marriages. Now what do you think might be an example of a marriage obligation? What are married people expected to do? Yes, Monica.

STUDENT 1: To take care of your marriage partner. . . .

TEACHER: Good. Anything else?

STUDENT 2: Uh . . . to take care of the children. . . .

TEACHER: Absolutely. Those are the main ones. So one obligation is to provide care for the children and provide them with an acceptable position in society. Now this definition of marriage says that marriage is a licensing of parenthood. OK, just what do we mean by that? A licensing of parenthood means it allows people to become parents. Now in most societies, the key has traditionally been having acceptable social fatherhood. This is called "social fatherhood" because traditionally the father is supposed to be responsible for ensuring the, uh . . . the social development of the child. Some people say, though, that this task has more often fallen to the mother. In addition, nowadays, some people prefer to use a term such as "social parenthood" and do away with the gender bias of the traditional term. . . . I, I see a question. Go ahead.

STUDENT 3: I'm a little confused by what you mean by social fatherhood or social parenthood. Could you explain more about that?

TEACHER: Sure. How about an example? Maybe that would make the idea clearer. In many countries, children can be adopted. Now in those cases, the adoptive parents are not the actual birth mother and father.

STUDENT 3: OK, so the people who adopt the child become the social mother and social father.

TEACHER: Exactly. So if you remember that the social mother or father isn't necessarily the birth mother or father, you'll have the idea.

STUDENT 3: OK.

TEACHER: All right. So those are a couple of ideas about marriage and how marriage can be defined. Now let's move on to take a look at how marriage partners are selected. The first ideas that are important are exogamy and endogamy. Exogamy. That's E-X-O-G-A-M-Y. And endogamy is spelled E-N-D-O-G-A-M-Y. Do you have that? OK . . . so exogamy is the idea that marriage should take place with someone from outside of our group and, uh . . . endogamy is the opposite . . . the idea that marriage should take place with someone inside our group.

Now this sounds quite simple, but if you think about it, any individual belongs to many different groups. For instance, we can belong to a racial group, a national group, a socioeconomic group, or a religious group, to name a few. So one idea of marriage might be that you should marry within your religious group. For instance, the parents of a Muslim child might want their child to marry another Muslim, parents of a Catholic another Catholic, and so on. What would that be? Exogamy or endogamy?

STUDENT 1: Endogamy. Uh . . . because that's inside a group. It's the same religion.

TEACHER: Right. Right. That's endogamy. However, those same parents would almost certainly demand that their child marry someone who was not a member of their immediate family. In other words, you can't marry your brother or sister. That's illegal in many societies. That's a fairly *universal* example of exogamy. Rules against marrying someone within one's own immediate family are thousands of years old.

If you think about your country, your culture, or your parents for a few minutes, you'll realize that endogamy is an extremely powerful idea in most societies. However, this concept is changing. Take my brother as an example, or I guess I should say a counter-example. What I mean is that his marriage is a good example of exogamy. He's married to a woman who is a different race and different nationality. They speak different native languages. Although our family has been understanding and supportive of his marriage, he's the only person in the entire family who has married outside of our national, cultural, and language group, so his marriage is far from the cultural *norm*. In many other parts of the world, the cultural norm as well is to marry within the national, racial, and linguistic group. This is interesting to think about, and I'll give you chances to discuss this later.

Now let's move on to the second point . . . about how marriage partners are selected. Who chooses the marriage partner. If we look at different cultures throughout the world, the decision is made either by the family—usually the parents—or by the couple who is getting married. The first case is called an arranged marriage. In an arranged marriage, the family *restricts* or controls the choice of marriage partner. In extreme cases, the individuals getting married don't meet each other until the wedding ceremony itself.

Obviously, there's no dating or romance before the wedding in this situation. Now, depending where you come from, you may be very familiar with arranged marriages because they're still common in the Middle East, Africa, and . . . uh, some countries in Asia. Arranged marriages are found in cultures in which the extended family is common. That is, the family is made up not only of parents and children, but also grandparents, grandchildren, and perhaps even aunts and uncles and so on. In extended families, marriage is a family affair, and individuals are expected to *conform* to the overall wishes of the group. In other words, the people getting married have little or no independence in terms of choosing their marriage partner.

Now, in contrast to arranged marriages, people in many places around the world have a great deal of freedom in deciding who they'll marry in what some call "love marriages." However, the notion that marriage is a private decision between two people is not a traditional idea. Typically, marriage has been the business of the whole family or even the whole tribe. This has been the norm throughout most of the world, and the idea that men and women could marry freely is relatively modern. In ancient societies, the tribe had to approve of the match, and the idea of a couple choosing each other freely would have been extremely shocking—and in many cases, against the law of the group. In other words, the wishes of the individual were *subordinate* to the wishes of the group. Even in the societies upon which modern western *civilization* is based, meaning the Romans and the Greeks, marrying for love was virtually unknown. The fact is, love has not been the point of marriage in much of human history. Having children and cementing ties between families, tribes, and other groups have been considered far more important. Actually, this all makes sense when you consider that marriage laws are essentially attempts to *preserve* the type of family unit that is valued in that culture and to protect traditional cultural values.

Now, let's fast-forward to the present. As we're all aware, the situation surrounding marriage has changed. The world has been *undergoing* rapid changes in the past century, and one of those changes has been a general *eroding* of the extended family in many parts of the world. The extended family is gradually being replaced with the smaller nuclear family, in which parents and children live separately from other members of the family. In the nuclear family, individual choice is very important. The idea is that *mature* individuals should make their own choices regarding marriage, and that love and romance are necessary conditions for a successful marriage. The couple is also expected to set up an independent household of their own. So, for better or worse, the world seems to be moving much more strongly toward freedom of choice where marriage is concerned. I think that it's interesting to *speculate* about the possible results of this trend. For instance, what do you think might happen where endogamy and exogamy are concerned? Do you think we may see a breakdown of endogamy? Will traditional institutions such as arranged marriages begin to erode? Do you think we'll see more interracial and international marriages? If so, how will this affect our world? Well,

I'd like to hear what you think about these ideas, so take a look at the discussion questions 2 through 5 at the end of Chapter 6, and be prepared to discuss those next class. All right. Any questions? . . . OK. Get out your homework and let's break into groups. . . .

Unit 6 Black Holes, White Holes, and Wormholes

TEACHER: Are there any questions before we begin? . . . No? . . . This afternoon I'm going to introduce you to three mysterious phenomena that have been puzzling astronomers since the early twentieth century—phenomena which promise to tell us a good deal about the origins of our universe and the nature of space and time. I'm talking about black holes, white holes, and wormholes. Are you familiar with these? I'm sure most of you have heard of these things—maybe through movies—but if you're like most people, you probably really don't understand them very well, right? What I'd like to talk about today—in pretty simple terms—is what these things are and what evidence we have that they exist.

Let me start, then, with black holes, which is probably the most familiar term for most people. The term "black hole" was first used back in 1969 by an American physicist named John Archibald Wheeler. He used it to describe the final stage in the life of very large stars. Black holes have incredibly strong gravitational force—so strong, in fact, that nothing can escape their gravity, not even light. And since no light can escape from them, and since we need light to see, we cannot see black holes, . . . which is precisely why we call them "*black* holes," right? . . . I see a question. Yes?

STUDENT 1: If they can't see them, how do scientists know black holes exist?

TEACHER: Excellent question. Scientists know they exist because they can see their effect on nearby objects. For example, black holes pull gases off the surface of nearby stars. Scientists are able to see these gases being sucked into the black hole.

STUDENT 1: I see . . .

TEACHER: So . . . what causes black holes? . . . Well, to answer that question it's helpful to first consider small and medium-sized stars. In the last stage of their lives, small and medium-sized stars become what we call white dwarfs. Now, a white dwarf is a small, very hot mass which is formed when the star's gravity *collapses* the star. All its heat, energy, and mass are compressed into a smaller and smaller space. This makes the star hotter and gives it a stronger gravitational pull. So that's what happens with small and medium-sized stars. As I've said, though, a black hole is the final stage in the life of a *very large* star, and this means its gravity's much stronger. Anyone like to suggest why? Sergio?

STUDENT 2: It's larger, so it has more mass, and that makes its gravitational pull stronger.

TEACHER: Yes, Sergio; you're absolutely right. In the case of a large star, there's more mass, and therefore the gravitational force is stronger. And, as the gravitational force becomes stronger and stronger, the star gets smaller and smaller until all its energy and mass is compressed into one tiny point called the "singularity"—that's "singularity." Got that? The singularity then sucks or pulls in everything near it–even light—because its gravitational force is so strong. So, we get a black hole. In other words, the powerful gravitational force of a black hole is caused by an extremely large mass being forced into—drawn into—a tiny space . . . the singularity. It's a bit like taking an orange and squeezing it so hard that it becomes as small as the head of a pin . . . but its weight doesn't change. When a large mass is forced into a tiny space like this, we say it's very dense. So, the tiny point called the singularity is an extremely dense object.

Now, here's an interesting question: How small does a star need to become in order to create the huge gravitational force of a black hole? Well, just consider this: We're told that if the sun were the size of a large mountain, it would need to *shrink* to the size of a small butterfly. Think about that—from a mountain to a small butterfly. Yet, it would still weigh the same as the original mountain. It would, as we've said, be extremely dense!

Now, most of their lives, stars remain a *constant* size because they have a balance of forces. On one side you've got heat—which is made because the star burns fuel, which helps push the star out. On the other side there's the effect of gravity, which pulls the star in. Heat versus gravity—see? So you get a balance. However, after billions of years, the star uses up all its fuel. Then, there's an imbalance—there's no more heat. Gravity wins the battle, and the star collapses.

Now, students often ask me what it would be like to be sucked into a black hole. The truth is we can't really be sure. However, scientists have tried to imagine this event, and it doesn't sound very appealing. Let me explain. The area immediately surrounding a black hole is called the "event horizon." Once you cross this area, the event horizon, you *can't* go back. The gravity there is so strong that you wouldn't be able to escape the black hole. The gravitational force pulling on your legs would be greater than the gravitational force pulling on your head, and the difference between the two forces would stretch you. Each and every atom of your body would be torn apart from the others and pulled toward the singularity at the black hole's center. There, they'd be squeezed until they *ceased* to exist. Not very nice!

OK, enough about what getting sucked into a black hole would be like. Now I'm going to move on to different types of black holes. Basically, there are two kinds of black holes: rotating and nonrotating. Let me explain the difference. If you cross the event horizon of a nonrotating black hole, it's certain you'll die. However, some scientists believe that this might not happen if you cross the event horizon of a rotating black hole. Because the hole *rotates*, you may be able to somehow avoid entering the singularity, and you may even be transported to another part of the universe and forced out of a white hole—although only as millions of particles probably. . . . Your body would have been torn apart, I'm afraid.

Now this brings us to our second and third phenomena: white holes and wormholes . . . things we know much less about and which are far more *controversial*. Basically, a white hole's the opposite of a black hole. Instead of matter being pulled into it, matter is pushed out of it. The idea is that if matter falls into a black hole, it comes out of a white hole at the other end—and matter in this case includes light, by the way. Light which enters a black hole exits *via* a white hole. This causes that white hole to appear as a bright white object—that's where it gets its name. Now, the actual tunnel through which the matter passes—from the black hole to the white hole—is called a "wormhole" . . . like a tunnel made by a worm. So you can see how the three phenomena are connected, right?

Now like I said, the idea of white holes and wormholes is still *very* uncertain. What I mean is there's no *empirical* evidence of their existence, it's all only theoretical. However, if a white hole and a black hole could be linked somehow, then whatever falls into a black hole could—in theory at least—suddenly appear out of a white hole some other place in the universe. Yes, Kristy? You have a question?

STUDENT 1: Uh, yeah . . . yeah, I do.

TEACHER: OK . . .

STUDENT 1: I once read a science-fiction novel about people using wormholes to travel through time. Is that right? I mean, is it possible to travel through time using wormholes?

TEACHER: Good question Kristy. The simple answer is . . . we don't know. You're right though; in science fiction, wormholes do allow people to travel across large amounts of space and time very quickly. If you want to understand how, just imagine an insect on a large piece of paper. It would take the insect a long time to walk across the paper, right? But if you folded the paper, the distance for the insect to cross would be much smaller, so it would cross the paper faster. Now wormholes bend space in the same way that you fold a piece of paper. This means that just as the insect never crosses most of the paper, someone traveling through a wormhole never passes through the space between the entrance and the exit. He, um . . . he basically takes a shortcut, not just through space—what we call the third dimension—but also through time—what we call the fourth dimension. And the exit point—the white hole—may be somewhere far away, possibly in a different universe . . . uh, linked to our own universe only via the wormhole. And if the exit to the wormhole is in the past, then you could travel back in time by going through. But, I repeat, this is more science fiction than reality, and many people *deny* the existence of wormholes. It's . . . yes?

STUDENT 1: But wait a minute. I thought wormholes had been proven mathematically.

TEACHER: True, it's been proven mathematically that they *could* exist. But that doesn't mean they actually exist in nature. And even if, one day, white holes and wormholes *were* shown to exist in reality, not just in theory, there'd still be at least two problems with traveling through them. For a start, scientists believe they wouldn't be *stable*. Therefore, even a small disturbance, like a person traveling through it, could cause the wormhole to collapse. In fact, some argue that, in order to travel through a wormhole, the black hole (the entry hole) and white hole (the exit hole) would have to be *identical*, and any small difference between them could destroy the wormhole. So that's problem number one. The second problem's this: Even if wormholes exist and are stable, chances are you'd be killed by the radiation inside them. So you see, although these are interesting *concepts*, right now it's difficult to know how real they are or how useful they might be to us.

All right, that's all I want to talk about today. I've tried to give you a simple introduction to three mysterious phenomena that astronomers are still trying to understand. Let me just recap some of my main points. I've said that black holes have incredibly strong gravity. That gravitational force pulls everything near a black hole into the tiny center of the hole called the singularity. When objects, including light, get squeezed into the singularity, they're destroyed. However, I made a distinction between rotating and nonrotating black holes. In the case of rotating black holes, if the object crosses the event horizon—the area just on the edge of a black hole—it may avoid the singularity and exit from a white hole in another part of the universe. This might, in theory, make time travel possible. You'll remember that a white hole is the opposite of a black hole; instead of sucking matter in, it forces matter out. And a wormhole is like a tunnel that connects the black hole and the white hole.

To wrap it up, I'll just say once again that there is evidence that black holes exist, even if we're not clear about how they work. We're much less certain, though, that white holes and wormholes exist—and if they do, what value they might be to mankind. One more thing to consider is this: If time travel *is* possible, then shouldn't we now be meeting people from the future? OK, that's it for today. Any questions?

Unit 7 Animal Talk

TEACHER: OK, let's get started . . . um, on today's topic of animal communication. I'm just wondering . . . how many of you have pets? Dogs, cats, birds, . . . any kind of pet. Quite a few, I see. In my case, I have a golden retriever. I'd certainly like to think that I'm able to communicate with him, but what kind of communication are we really engaging in? Actually, this is a very interesting and controversial question because, in many ways, it's difficult to compare animals and humans. Humans are one species, and there are many *species* of animals. And each species has its own way of communicating, and some of those forms of communication are completely different from what we use. For instance, some types of fish use electrical currents to communicate, some insects use vibrations, and bats use ultrasonic signals. And then there's the sense of smell. Even though humans try to cover natural body odors with soap and deodorant and perfume, odor is a common method of communicating for many animals.

So . . . you see, animal communication is really not very *straightforward*, so today I would like to simplify matters. Although we acknowledge the fact that animals communicate in many different ways, today we're only going to consider whether animals can use language as we know it—in other words, language that is composed of words and that has a grammar. Today, now I'd like to consider three questions. First, what do animal sounds mean? Second, do animals intend to communicate? And third, do animals speak in sentences?

All right. The first question that I just mentioned was what animal sounds mean. Now to understand this, we need to take a close look at different types of communication. These can be divided into two types: affective communication and symbolic communication. Affective communication involves the communication of emotion. Humans use affective communication when we laugh, uh, when we cry . . . and, um, much of our nonverbal communication is this affective communication. We show a great deal of feeling with our facial expressions, gestures, and so on. Of course, animals can also express emotion, and this is one of the reasons why we love our pets so much—they're expressive in many ways. Dogs, in particular, are popular in many cultures because they're so good at appearing happy, pained, and sad. They even seem to mirror human feelings. For instance, when I'm feeling down or I've had a hard day, my dog becomes quiet and actually looks a little sad or tired himself. Well, that's my experience, but, in any case, almost all scientists agree that most higher order animals like dogs and cats can use affective communication. So one answer to our first question is that many animal sounds communicate what we can call an emotional state.

Now, remember that I said there is a second type of communication—symbolic. Symbolic communication is information about a specific referent that can be encoded by a signaler and decoded by a receiver. Now that's rather complicated, so let me give you an example. If I say the word "Brazil," the referent in this case is the actual country, Brazil, because I'm referring to the country. I encode this referent with a set of sounds. If you understand that referent and the set of sounds, then you'll be able to decode or translate the sounds and understand the referent. That is, you'll understand that I'm talking about a country in South America. Now can animals do that? Well, the answer appears to be "yes." But because their vocabularies are so limited, it's probably safe to say that they can use very little symbolic communication. For instance, scientists have *confirmed* that one type of monkey in Africa, the vervet monkey, clearly makes different alarm calls. One type of call is very general and seems to communicate the idea of "Watch out!" or "Stay alert!" Monkeys that hear this call begin to look around more and act more careful. They're less *tranquil*, less relaxed than usual, and they're less willing to leave the safety of nearby trees. Other calls, now, are quite specific. There's a call that monkeys use when they see a leopard, a different call for eagles, and yet a different call for snakes. Now the interesting thing is that there's every indication that monkeys use these calls in a symbolic way. For instance, when a vervet monkey hears a leopard call, it often runs for a particular type of tree that leopards can't climb easily. When the monkeys hear an eagle alarm call, they immediately stop what they're doing and begin scanning the sky. When they hear the snake call, they stand up straight and scan the ground in the immediate area.

Now in addition to alarm calls, animals such as monkeys and birds use food calls. Now these calls not only let others know that food has been found, but they can also sometimes give information about how much and what quality of food has been found. Now another interesting point, which is not well understood, is that some animals such as chickens seem to use food calls *deceptively*. In other words, sometimes chickens will use a call to indicate that they have found food even when they haven't. So what does this mean? Do chickens lie? Are they intentionally *deceitful*? This is a sophisticated use of communication, but few scientists are willing to admit that chickens are consciously trying to deceive other chickens, because they don't appear to have the intelligence for that kind of thinking.

The second question concerns whether animals actually intend to communicate. In other words, do animals care if there is another animal nearby who will hear their call? Well, the answer is "yes." It appears that animals do care about this. Wild birds call out when they spot something important like food or an enemy, but they only do this when other birds are present. On the other hand, they're frequently silent in the same situations when no other birds of their species are around. So birds are apparently aware of their own species. Gender is also a factor here. For example, male chickens will call out more often when female chickens are nearby, and there's even a difference depending on whether the chicken is known or unknown. The male chickens will use food calls most frequently when unknown female chickens are nearby. Uh, I guess I should also mention that this phenomenon is not just limited to birds or chickens. Chimpanzees also communicate far more when other chimps or, in some cases, when humans are present. So the general answer to the second question is "yes." It does appear that at least some types of animals are sensitive to the presence of an audience and that they do intend to communicate.

Now I've told you we believe that some animals, such as certain monkeys, can use something like words—in a limited way. You'll remember, I mentioned it appears that they can say something like "eagle," "leopard," or "snake." But humans can use grammar, so we communicate different meanings by using words in different *sequences*. So for instance, I can say "The dog bit the man" and that has one meaning. But if I use the same words and change the sequence and say "The man bit the dog," now I have communicated a very different meaning. Well, this last question is about whether animals can do this too. In other words, can they use some form of grammar? What do you think? Well, the answer is that there is no recorded natural example of animals making anything like a sentence or using the order of a sequence of sounds to communicate symbolic meaning. The monkeys and birds we've been talking about can make alarm calls or food calls quickly or slowly, loudly or softly, but they never seem to *manipulate* the sequence.

Even the birds that seem to be saying "a lot of good food" are communicating that idea with one *identical* call that doesn't change. They're not using grammar as far as anyone can tell.

Now, one group of animals that is able to manipulate their language is songbirds. As you are probably aware, many wild birds sing rather complex birdsongs. And these songs are created by combining a variety of notes in many different patterns. Some birds have hundreds of phrases that they use in thousands of different combinations. However, *contrary* to what you might believe, there is absolutely no evidence whatsoever that birds can communicate any symbolic meaning by manipulating these musical notes and phrases. Instead, they seem to use their songs just as a way of advertising themselves, attracting a mate, or maybe even expressing some type of emotion.

Well, now today we began with three questions, and I'd like to return to those questions once again. First, what do animal sounds mean? In most cases, we think they communicate what we would call emotion, or affective meaning; but in some cases, they stand for specific things in the environment such as food and the presence of danger. Second, do animals consciously intend to communicate? Well, generally I suppose the answer is "yes," though having an audience that understands the message is an important factor. And third, do animals use grammar? Here the answer seems to be "no." If animals use some type of grammar, it's nothing that scientists have been able to identify and confirm. One reason for this is that using grammar requires far more mental processing and far more sophisticated memory than using a simple vocabulary with no grammar, and this may be the obstacle for animals—they don't have the brainpower. Some animals do have the brainpower to use a very limited number of individual words in a *rigid*, inflexible way, but they can't acquire thousands and thousands of words like human beings and then manipulate those words using grammar.

The thing that really sets humans apart from animals is our incredible ability to use language symbolically, produce the same words in many different combinations, and assign different meanings to those combinations. In short, grammar is an *innovation* that only humans have been able to develop. So, although I might prefer to believe that when I get home tonight my dog will say something like "Nice to see you; let's go outside and play Frisbee," he's probably really communicating something more like "happy, happy" or "hungry, hungry." But I'll settle for that because we communicate pretty well with each other. All right. Now that's it for today. Are there any questions? No? OK. Will you please read Chapters 6 and 7 before next class, and I'll see you then.

Unit 8 Gender Differences in Language

TEACHER: Morning, everyone. You'll recall we began looking at gender differences last week, and I'd like to continue that theme today and focus on male and female communication styles—the differences between the way men and women communicate. Let me start by saying the issue of gender differences in communication seems to be an interesting one for most people—certainly for most students. Anyone like to suggest why?

STUDENT 1: I think because most of us are looking for partners, a long-term love relationship . . . you know? So it helps to understand the opposite sex, so we can communicate with them better.

TEACHER: Well, that probably is one major reason—so we can get along better. The truth is, gender differences have fascinated mankind for as long as people have been writing down their thoughts, from as far back as the story of Adam and Eve to *contemporary* books. And although numerous books and articles have been written on the subject, almost all of them draw the same conclusion: Men and women speak different languages. I'll bet most of us here have read or at least heard of some book that talks about why men and women can't talk to each other, or how they can improve communication with the opposite sex. Of course, this isn't really surprising. Most of us want to relate better to the opposite sex, and most of us have a sense that there are differences in communication style, even if they're simply based on *stereotypes*. As a matter of fact, research based on transcribed speech—that is, speech which has been recorded and written down exactly as it was spoken—shows that both sexes can generally tell whether a speaker is male or female. So clearly, gender differences in language really do exist. After all, let's face it, men and women have been misunderstanding each other for generations, and that leads to problems in love relationships, challenges in professional life . . . uh . . . the workplace, and so on. Just think about this for a minute, if you will: Researchers claim we spend 70 percent of our working hours communicating and 30 percent of that is talking. So you can see it's essential that we learn how to communicate with each other. There are more complex reasons, though, why studying communication is important. The fact is . . . the fact . . . you need to realize that communication's not simply a matter of saying what you mean and being understood. *How* we say what we mean is equally *crucial* because it influences the way people perceive and respond to us. And how we express ourselves, our style, says a lot about how we see our own status—our power, our authority, if you like—in relation to our listeners. We adjust . . . we change the way we talk depending on who we're talking to and the *impression* we want to give them. In other words, our communicative style is socially conditioned. Think about that. Our communication style is socially conditioned. How we use language with others is a learned behavior, and how we talk and listen are deeply influenced by cultural expectations. Problems arise because women and men are like people who have grown up in two different subcultures. They have two broadly different styles of speaking and establishing social status based on how they've grown up. What I'd like to do now is look at how these different styles develop.

There have been many attempts to explain gender differences in communication styles, with genetics and the environment both at the top of the list. In the case of **inherent** genetic factors, some suggest that differences in men and women's brain structure and hormone production contribute to differences in thought processes, and these in turn contribute to different behavior between the sexes. Precisely how much influence genetic factors have on communication compared to the environment—that's to say, how much communication style is a product of *nature* as opposed to *nurture*—is not yet clear. Uh . . . nevertheless, evidence suggests that nature's responsible for only 1 percent of the difference in communication style between the sexes. Think about it—only 1 percent! That means the environment plays a far bigger role. Now let's stop and consider just what that means. Generally speaking, boys and girls tend to participate in different kinds of activities as children. These activities reflect the everyday activities of adult men and women. Girls dress baby dolls and boys build things, for example. Toy stores know this very well. Now this is a generalization, of course—there are girls who love building block sets like LEGO, for example—but just look at how toy stores arrange their toys according to activities for girls and activities for boys. And as a result of their different activities, boys and girls develop different communication styles. Girls traditionally practice more intimacy-related skills, and learn how to relate to others. That is, they use language to *establish* intimacy, as a basis of friendship. Their style is what some writers call "collaboration-oriented." When girls play house, for instance, this type of play naturally produces more collaborative communication—discussions based on relationships, and so on. Boys, on the other hand, tend to be more goal-driven or task-oriented, and practice work-related skills. They might discuss, for example, how to build a castle or lay out a track, and how to get the job done. They're encouraged more to compete with others and generally use language to establish their status in the group. You could say that their communication style is "competition-oriented" rather than collaboration-oriented.

Evidence suggests that these patterns are **reinforced** when children socialize with their peers. Of course, parents, teachers, and others help establish these patterns of communication in boys and girls by directing children's activities. They buy boys construction-type gifts and girls domestic gifts, for instance. But they also do it subconsciously by talking to boys and girls in different ways. For example, if their children have problems, mothers tend to regulate or guide their children more than fathers . . . and they tend to be more controlling with their daughters than with their sons. Fathers, in contrast, tend to be more concerned with identifying the problem quickly and demanding a solution—and they tend to do this more with their sons than with their daughters. So the mothers tend to be more controlling and have more rules, and the fathers tend to be more demanding of solutions. So as a result, when they are adults, men and women tend to *exhibit* differences in their styles of communication.

But what are these differences? Well, at a general level, there are differences in the purpose of communication— why they talk. We could say that generally men talk to give information or to report—they're "goal-oriented." They focus on solving problems and are less likely to ask for help or directions—maybe because traditional social roles demand that men behave like leaders, as being in control— whether they feel that way or not. As a general rule, men try to establish status, their level of authority in a situation, but women try to establish and support intimacy, or close relationships with others. This might well be because, until recently, it was the man who was typically in the more competitive environment—both at work and at play—and therefore who may have been more concerned about establishing, maintaining, and increasing status. Today, of course, that's changing, and this can be seen in the type of topics men and women discuss. Let's consider that next as we look at some slightly more detailed observations about gender differences in communication.

At the risk of stereotyping, I'll say that women have tended to discuss topics related to relationships, such as the home, clothes, and so on. Men, on the other hand, have tended to discuss money or business. However, that trend appears to be changing, with women talking more about work and money—no doubt due to changing social roles and the fact that more women are working. Actually, one study found that the percentage of women's conversations *devoted* to work and money rose from 3.7 percent in 1922 to 37.5 percent in 1990. That's more than a 33 percent jump. That speaks volumes, doesn't it?

Given the collaboration/competition distinction I mentioned earlier, you probably won't be surprised to learn that men tend to be more aggressive and argumentative than women, and use more expletives—strong language, in other words. They want to get their point across. Also as you might expect, women are more successful with interpersonal tasks, it seems—in particular, comforting, persuading, and justifying decisions. They also tend to be better listeners than men. One aspect of this is *how* they listen; according to various studies, in conversations women use more "mm-hmm," "rights," and so on, to *show* they're listening.

And what about nonverbal communication? Well, women show greater skills in sending and understanding nonverbal messages. Also, they're less likely to signal dominance. Typical male body language, on the other hand— wide gestures, sitting with knees apart, and so on—often displays status and dominance by increasing personal space. Finally, men tend to stammer more than women and use more "ums" and "uhs" when they speak. They're more restless, use more hand gestures in conversation, and tend to speak too loudly.

Now, before I finish, a few final thoughts for you to go away with. As I've said, male/female communication styles are mainly a social phenomenon. Given that society's constantly changing, we can also expect communication styles to change to reflect the changing roles of men and women. More women, for example, are working and rising to positions of power and authority in business, and this is changing how they communicate. Likewise, as men take on more domestic duties—take more responsibility for things like raising children, for example—their style's also changing. I've heard it said that language has prevented women from taking on new roles in society and achieving true equality with men. One way to deal with this may be for parents to change—or at least vary the kinds of activities they encourage their children to *engage in*. This will change the way parents talk to their children and therefore children's own ideas about how they should speak. Perhaps we also need to reduce gender *segregation*—get boys and girls playing together more—so they develop more similar styles. In other words, the way we bring up and educate our children is important. In fact, the changes could be quite *dramatic*!

I'd like to close by adding two final words of caution. Firstly, when we talk about male and female differences of any kind, it's easy to fall into the trap of stereotyping men and women. Stereotypes are based on generalizations—which, of course, do not apply to everyone. What's more, even if generalizations are accurate enough at one point in time, society changes, as we've seen, and it may take some time for the ideas behind the generalizations to reflect those changes. And secondly, please bear in mind that when we talk about male and female communication styles, we have to understand that these vary from culture to culture—not surprising given the role of socialization. Therefore, most of the things I've been saying apply to North American culture but might not apply to all cultures. OK, that's it for today.

Unit 9 Fashion and Status

TEACHER: Today, everyone, as part of our look at fashion and design, we're going to take a look at fashion and social status, that is, how we use fashion to make statements about our social status—who we are, how wealthy we are, and so on. We do this with the kinds of cars we buy, the style of our houses, and of course the clothes we wear, which is the subject of today's discussion.

Now, the idea of using special clothes to signal social status has a long history, dating back to ancient Egypt. In very *hierarchical* societies like ancient Egypt, for example, only those in high positions could wear sandals. Also, the Greeks and Romans had laws which controlled the type, the color and number of garments that could be worn, as well as the kind of embroidery used. These were known as sumptuary laws . . . that's S-U-M-P-T-U-A-R-Y . . . sumptuary laws. . . . However, as barriers between social classes became weaker, these so-called sumptuary laws became increasingly difficult to enforce and were eventually *abandoned*. Instead, high status was indicated by the cost of a person's clothing—you know, rich and exotic materials, expensive and often unnecessary accessories . . . and, um, difficult-to-care-for styles. This kind of expensive and often unnecessary clothing was designed to attract attention; it was an example of what's called conspicuous consumption—that's conspicuous consumption. And of course, people thought the type of clothes you wore reflected what you could afford; in other words, your clothes reflected your wealth. I'm going to be using this

word *"conspicuous"* a lot today—conspicuous basically means deliberately attracting attention.

If you look at fashion today, things haven't really changed much, have they? Even though people these days don't dress in silver or gold lace, clothes are still very much a sign of status. In fact, you could say that nowadays many people believe clothes tell us about the personality—the honesty, talent, and intelligence of the person wearing them. In some social circles, there's often a feeling that someone who's not well dressed is probably dishonest or stupid, and without talent. Now that's sad but true, I'm afraid. Many of us make these judgments very quickly and unconsciously, . . . which, of course, is why people read and write books with titles like *Dress for Success*. The idea is if you dress well, people will judge you positively even before you open your mouth, right? I'd say that people have very *definite* ideas about dress and character.

But today I'm going to look in detail at this idea of conspicuous consumption. So just to recap, let me repeat that conspicuous consumption is about the different ways we spend money in order to show people our wealth. Mmm? And one of the most obvious ways we do this is by wearing more clothes than other people. This is sometimes called conspicuous addition. Whatever the occasion, the well-to-do normally wear more clothes. In North America, for instance, men are more likely to wear jackets and vests, and women, pantyhose, scarves, and unnecessary but expensive wraps—even in mid-summer. And on the beach, even though their swimsuits may be like everyone else's, just watch the wealthy put on their silk beach kimonos when they come out of the water . . . or maybe a shirt, hat, and bag that matches their swimsuit. And people notice, right? Of course, they're supposed to notice; that's the point.

Of course, people also show off their status by wearing a lot of clothes *consecutively* rather than *simultaneously*. In other words, as we've seen, people wear more clothes, but they also like to show off, to display as many different outfits as possible. Basically, the more outfits you wear, the higher your status; it's as simple as that. Now how do people do this? Well, they divide daily life into different sorts of activities—what's been called conspicuous division—and each of these activities, such as going to work or going out to dinner, requires a different kind of clothing. Now, this isn't anything new. In the nineteenth and early twentieth centuries, it was common for the wealthier classes to have different clothing for different parts of the day. Men would wear a morning suit, a dress coat, um, a dinner jacket, and women, morning clothes, walking clothes, tea gowns, um, motoring outfits, evening dresses. . . . You name it, there was a costume for it.

Now today, we have the same tradition, but the emphasis is on sports rather than social life. Fashionable people will have different outfits for different sports, whether it's jogging, hiking, cycling, golf, or aerobics—and to wear the wrong outfit can cause a loss of *prestige*. . . . This, by the way, is what enables manufacturers of sports equipment to make so much money. And it's not just having *separate* clothing that's important, it's also having the *right* equipment; that also has to be high prestige. . . . It's important to have the correct brand names.

Now another way of indicating high status is to own many similar garments so that you rarely wear the same thing. This is what's known as conspicuous multiplication. For instance, some very wealthy men wear a brand new shirt every day; they'll never use the same shirt twice. Having a large, up-to-date wardrobe is especially important for men and women who want to establish themselves socially and professionally . . . uh, you know, who, um, . . . who want to make an impression. Once people know them . . . have made a decision about their status, it usually becomes less important. Teenagers in particular feel very strongly about showing variety in their dress. For example, teenage girls often feel so embarrassed about wearing the same outfit twice in the same week, that even if they only own a few clothes, they'll try hard to make them *seem* new by combining them in different ways and with different accessories. They feel so strongly about this, in fact, that they'll often prefer quantity to quality.

Now, uh, let's move on to another form of conspicuous consumption, and I'm talking about the use of expensive materials, conspicuous materials. Now, in the past, materials such as satin and velvet were prestigious because they were handwoven and required a lot of time and labor. But today, modern machinery's changed all that. The result is that natural materials which are often more *scarce* are now more prestigious. I'm talking about materials like silk, leather, wool. In today's world, natural is best. Artificial materials, such as nylon and polyester, were expensive and very fashionable when they first appeared, but as they became cheaper to produce, "polyester" became a dirty word, and now it's seen as the poor man's silk. You can also see a similar pattern with animal skins and pelts. Today because wildlife's becoming *scarcer*, these things have gotten more expensive and therefore more prestigious, particularly the hides of animals like the alligator. In centuries past, however, when things were different, skins and pelts of more common animals were associated with peasants and shepherds and hunters—even outlaws. To show their status, merchants wore robes trimmed with less common fur such as beaver, noblemen preferred sable, and kings and queens wore ermine—all, again, relatively rare materials, and therefore indicators of status. As you know though, even though skins of wild animals are often prestigious in the sense of being rare and therefore expensive, today they're also seen as showing a disregard for the environment and wildlife.

OK. Now another way people display their wealth is by wearing jewelry . . . high-priced stones and metals—particularly those like gold and diamonds whose market price is generally *known* to be high. Gemstones such as rubies or emeralds, whose market price is less well known or which are more easily imitated, are less popular. Instant identification's desirable, you see. In other words, people need to be able to understand, just by looking, that something's expensive. And that's why platinum never really became very popular. Even though it's more expensive than gold, the problem was people couldn't easily tell it from silver or aluminum. Anyway, we call this display of expensive items conspicuous wealth.

Next, we come to conspicuous labeling. Not long ago, you could recognize a high-quality hand-tailored suit made in, say, London's Saville Row or Paris. Today, though, thanks to sophisticated manufacturing methods and artificial materials that look like the real thing, it's become very difficult to tell simply by looking whether a suit, jacket, or whatever has been handmade using the finest natural materials, and therefore whether it has cost far more than your average, off-the-rack equivalent. In addition, more people than ever are wealthy. Together, these two things create a problem. It's almost impossible to distinguish the rich from the very rich simply by looking at what they're wearing. So how do the very rich show their status? Well, one way is by using labels to show expensive brands. Designers realized that high-status garments didn't need to be recognizably of better quality or more difficult to produce than other garments; they only needed to be recognizably more *expensive*. So, they had to somehow include the price of each garment in the basic design. How did they do that? The answer is they moved the designer's name from the inside to the outside of the garment. Simple! Then they aggressively promoted these names and trademarks until they became household names. Now the prices of these designer garments were not high because they were better quality, but because of the huge cost of advertising them. And people wearing these clothes would be sending out the message, "I can afford to buy clothes made by this designer." In fact, people will happily buy *inferior* quality clothes if they're clearly labeled and everyone knows they are highly priced . . . and cotton T-shirts are a great example of this. They may fade quickly and shrink out of shape after just a few washings, but it doesn't matter. If they have the right designer name printed on them, people prefer them to better-made T-shirts. Apparently, they make the people who wear them feel "secure"; at least, that's what research indicates. Conspicuous labeling, then, was a *radical* but very effective solution to a rather difficult problem. Do you see how this works?

Now to wrap up, I'd like to mention two other kinds of conspicuous consumption in clothing, to bring our total to eight different types. One of these is conspicuous outrage—in other words, dressing which leads people to feel outrage . . . shock, if you like. Here, people purposely wear clothes that aren't in good taste, that others won't approve of . . . that don't *conform*. These clothes attract negative attention, but they get attention nonetheless. Now the teenage punks of the 1980s were a good example of this, as are pop stars who turn up at formal events in, you know, torn or faded T-shirts with, uh, offensive language printed on them.

Now this brings me to the last type: what I call associative consumption, in which people wear items of clothing because they've acquired prestige through association with high-status individuals—such as royalty like Princess Diana or film stars. A good example of this is, um, John Lennon's round glasses. These became a fashion icon, and even today people refer to round glasses as John Lennon glasses. Associative consumption also includes high-status activities. Just think of the clothing associated with horseback riding—checked suits, glossy high-heeled boots, polo shirts, and waisted jackets. These items have the power of association. We may assume that the people wearing them ride and own horses and therefore have the money associated with these activities. The same's true of fashion goods associated with golfing and yachting. They all send out strong signals.

OK . . . so let's quickly review. We've said that conspicuous consumption's a way of signaling how wealthy we are, what status we have, and clothing's one way we do this . . . it's one way we consume conspicuously. I've mentioned conspicuous addition, meaning people wear more clothes to show their status. And then we looked at conspicuous division, where people wear different outfits at different times of the day or for different activities. And then there was conspicuous multiplication, where people have many garments of the same type. And then we considered conspicuous materials, in which people wear rare or expensive materials to show wealth, followed by conspicuous wealth, where people wear high-priced materials such as gold and diamonds, usually as accessories. And after that, we looked at conspicuous labeling, where garments are worn with their designer labels on the outside for everyone to see—not too subtle, but it works. It says something. And finally, we looked at conspicuous outrage—where clothing is used to attract negative attention, where the intent is to shock people—and associative consumption, where clothing is associated with a celebrity or lifestyle.

So you see, fashion really is a *vehicle* for self-expression, for saying, "This is me and this is the kind of lifestyle I have. Can you match it?" All right everyone, let's take a break there and we'll start our seminar in fifteen minutes, OK?

Unit 10 The Making of Genius

TEACHER: Hello, everyone. Today we'll, uh . . . begin our next unit, and the topic is one that I think you'll find interesting. One of the most noteworthy aspects of human beings is our remarkable ability to learn a wide variety of skills, and to learn some skills very well. I'm sure you'll agree that great athletes, musicians, and singers are often the objects of our respect and admiration, and one reason for this is that many of us believe these individuals are special, that is, we believe that they have special talents provided by their DNA. They are gifted. But do you think it is really true? Could you or I become another Mozart, another Einstein, or another Van Gogh? Today we'll look at this question by discussing expert performance, that is, performances that are at a world-class level. First, I'd like to focus on the importance of practice and some reasons why many scientists doubt that *innate* talent is particularly important in skill development. Second, we'll look at the contribution which innate talent might make, and finally, I'll try to tie these two ideas together by proposing that it's the interaction of practice and talent that produces great musicians, scientists, and so on.

OK, so let's begin . . . let's begin with the notion of practice. First of all, let's consider the fact that there've been historical increases in performance in many areas, particularly in the past 1 to 200 years. For instance, Olympic records in many sports have been broken repeatedly, even in sports

that've had few changes in equipment, such as running sports. How can we account for this? Well, if innate talent were a strongly limiting factor, we wouldn't expect such rapid improvements in world record performances, unless you happen to believe that innate talent has increased in the past century. Of course, no one believes this to be the case. Instead, we believe that external factors, such as better training methods and better diets, have had an *enormous* effect.

Now this phenomenon isn't just limited to athletics. We can find the same situation in the world of music. There are pieces of music that used to be thought of as being virtually unplayable. For instance, in the nineteenth century some people thought that the violinist Niccolò Paganini had magical powers because of the difficult techniques he had mastered. However, today many of his pieces are regularly played by adult and even by outstanding child musicians, so once again the general conclusion is that innate talent hasn't limited human performance to this point in history. If that's right, then it's reasonable to expect that better practice and training will allow skill levels to continue to rise. . . . Yeah? Do you have a question?

STUDENT: I have a comment. I mean, what you're saying makes sense to me because every year new world records are broken. I don't think we really know what our *limitations* are.

TEACHER: I agree. We're getting closer to human limitations every time a new world record is set, but you're right—we're not there yet. Now . . . um . . . another reason to believe that practice is extremely important is because general *intelligence* and memory abilities and specific—I mean, specific—abilities are not strongly related. I see a question.

STUDENT: Sorry to interrupt again, but I'm not sure what you mean by "not strongly related."

TEACHER: OK. Here's an example. World chess masters are intelligent, but they're not any more intelligent than many people who can't play chess at all. When world-class chess players have been tested for general memory skills, their memories are no better than many nonexperts, but when they're tested for their memory of board positions in chess, they have an extremely well-developed memory of chess board positions that they've seen in the past. This allows them to make decisions more rapidly and accurately than ordinary people.

STUDENT: OK, so experts have a . . . a . . . a kind of specialized type of knowledge . . . or a specialized memory.

TEACHER: Well, specialized knowledge. In the case of chess, a major part of that specialized knowledge is their specialized memory for chess board positions. OK? And it all comes from enormous amounts of practice and experience in their area. Now a third point is that success is based on a variety of motivational, personality, and social factors. Important personality factors are . . . let's see . . . perseverance, or you might say patience in the face of failure, the ability to concentrate for long periods of time, self-confidence, optimism, . . . uh . . . competitiveness, a high energy level, and . . . um . . . the ability to control anxiety. Now related to this is the idea of social *support*. Remember that I just mentioned the ability to concentrate for long periods of time. Well, research has shown that very few people have the ability to practice *intensely* for long periods of time when they have no social support. An example might help here. We know that sustained support from an adult is needed for young musicians to become successful, because without a lot of support and encouragement, young people won't do the long hours of practice necessary to excel. In other words, parental support seems to come first, and this is followed by intense practice, which then sometimes results in great skill development.

Now I've mentioned that in order to become an exceptional performer in a complex skill like playing the violin, a person has to work hard for a long period of time. Now what do you think I might mean by that? Is a long period of time one year? Three years? Five years? What do you think? . . . Yes, Greg?

STUDENT: Well, I would say a lot longer than five years. I've read about the lives of several famous musicians and athletes and writers, and . . . uh, I don't know, they have to practice maybe eight or ten years or so.

TEACHER: Ten years is the answer. The truth is that even the most talented people need to begin to study or practice before the age of six, and then put in more than ten years of intensive, high-quality practice. Let's look at the classic example of a genius, Wolfgang Amadeus Mozart. Behind the original, creative music that he wrote was years of hard work. Mozart practiced intensely. He wrote his first seven works for the piano and orchestra when he was between the ages of eleven and sixteen. Now that's impressive, but they were actually arrangements of works by other composers, so his early works were a kind of practice, not creative or original. Mozart didn't produce an original masterpiece for piano and orchestra until he was twenty-one. But think about that. By the time he was twenty-one, he had been playing music for sixteen years and had been writing music for piano and orchestra for ten years—so even in Mozart's case, a long period of practice preceded his works of creative genius.

All right. So far I've suggested that three things are necessary to become great: practice, strong personal characteristics such as self-confidence, and strong social support. But let's consider another factor—innate talent. This is the idea that our genetic qualities are important, that we inherit talent from our parents. Right away, I'd like to point out that the effects of innate talent are extremely difficult to measure and separate from environmental factors. Even in cases in which young children are very skilled, it's not clear that innate talent is the main cause, because researchers have almost always discovered that the child's parents had created a powerful supportive environment for the child from infancy, so social support and encouragement probably played important roles.

Now something that may surprise you is that most people who become highly skilled as adults don't show signs of greatness when they're young children. In one study, a researcher looked at twenty-one Americans who were beginning careers as concert pianists. Generally, the signs of special skill followed a combination of good opportunities and strong encouragement from parents and teachers. Signs of greatness couldn't be seen until they had practiced intensely for at least six years. The same results were found for professional tennis players in Germany, and that's a country that has produced top players such as Steffi Graf. Signs of innate talent usually only come out after long-term parental encouragement and a considerable amount of training.

Notwithstanding the difficulties involved with trying to *detect* innate talent, many child psychologists believe that some children are born with talent that allows them to learn specific skills very rapidly. An example of a skill that can clearly be inherited is working memory *capacity*, that is, a person's ability to process and hold information in the memory when solving problems. This type of ability seems to be important in young people who are especially good at mathematics. In addition, some degree of general intelligence, such as the capacity to analyze problems, is clearly inherited. So some aspects of intelligence do seem to be innate.

Now, another way in which innate talents may play a role is related to what I said earlier about personality factors such as self-confidence, *persistence*, and competitiveness. Many researchers believe that these qualities are at least partially innate. For instance, some children seem to have a natural ability to concentrate intensely for long periods. Others seem to be naturally daring and confident. Some seem to be born with the physical, mental, and emotional energy necessary to achieve greatness. That may be a fundamental part of innate talent.

A further point is that most researchers have partly defined innate ability as the ability for someone to perform a skill well before getting the opportunity for much practice. For example, now if you find that a child is good at playing the piano right away, without any practice, you might assume that the child has innate skills. However, this may not be the case. What we should perhaps be looking at in young people is not great ability when they begin their training, but rather ease of learning. Ease of learning may be the most important sign that a child is gifted. I'm sure you noticed in school that some children seemed to learn to play a sport, play a musical instrument, or do mathematics more easily than others. It seems reasonable that this is a sign of innate talent.

OK, to summarize, what does all this mean? Well, it looks like becoming great at something involves a fairly predictable process. First, the person is born with certain personality characteristics. These characteristics are then probably nurtured by the child's parents. Next, when the child begins to show interest in some area, the parents react supportively—that is, they encourage and perhaps even push the child to work hard and to practice intensively. Then the child goes on to achieve increasingly higher levels of skill. As the child becomes more skilled, he or she becomes more motivated to excel, and parents and teachers provide support. This can result in a long-term commitment to practice. Finally, if the child continues to work hard for around ten years, he or she will probably become very highly skilled in the area chosen.

Now I'd like to remind you that scientific research rarely allows us to understand how to separate genetic and external factors in human learning. What I'd like to suggest, though, is that these two accounts of skill development are not *incompatible*. To *quote* a line on page 343 of your textbook: "It's quite likely that the interaction of innate capacities and opportunities for engaging in intense training result in high levels of performance." I think those words sum up the situation quite accurately.

In closing, I'd like to ask you a final question. Were the works of Mozart brought into this world only through practice and study? Can anyone make the scientific breakthroughs of Einstein or play basketball like Michael Jordan if they work hard enough? In my opinion, they cannot. Innate talent is also needed, but we just haven't learned how to measure it yet. All right, now I'd like you to get into groups. Look at page 349, and there . . .

Unit 11 The New Global Superculture

TEACHER: Morning. I'd like to begin today's lecture with a question, and the question's this: We are now in an age where powerful social, political, and technological forces are changing our world and rapidly creating a *homogeneous* global society where people think and behave in similar ways. Do you think it's possible, in this kind of global society, for individual cultures to survive? Or will their unique traditions gradually disappear? And if these unique traditions were to disappear, would it really matter? Would it, as many believe, really be a tragedy if we were to lose those things that make societies, communities, different? The fact is, the world is losing cultures quicker than you might think. Language is the best measure of cultural diversity, and it's estimated that one language is dying every two weeks, and with it unique ways of life . . . ways of thinking, communicating, and living.

So that's today's theme—the issue, if you will—that's at the heart of everything I'm going to say. First, I'll try to identify . . . um . . . describe the forces that are pushing us, driving us toward a homogeneous global society, a world superculture. Then, we'll go on to consider the disadvantages of a homogeneous society, and I'll . . . um . . . offer some thoughts as to why we should think very seriously about *preserving* individual cultures and their traditions.

So . . . why is a global superculture emerging? What factors can we say have contributed? Well, to start with, there's flight. You often hear people say the world has become smaller, and without doubt, flight—particularly affordable air travel—has had the greatest influence here. This means the airplane caused not just a technological but also a social revolution. Suddenly, large numbers of ordinary people were able to interact with people from other cultures thousands of miles away and see with their own eyes the differences and the similarities between them, the things that

make people human regardless of culture. Now think about it. Many of us in this room have, I'm sure, traveled to parts of the world our parents or grandparents never dreamed of visiting. And, as a consequence of air travel, commercial links, overseas businesses, and so on have become far easier to establish, so now goods, technologies, and fads are entering new markets faster than ever before. Can anybody think of a good example of something—say, a technology or fad—that's spread quickly?

STUDENT: How about cell phones? Everybody's got them now.

TEACHER: Great example, Adam. OK, Let's take the cell phone for instance. You could go to any country in the world today, developed or otherwise, and I'd bet you could find a cell phone. You might have to search a bit, but I'm sure you could find one. Yet these haven't been around very long, relatively speaking, right? Same with computers. That's to say, because people from diverse cultures are able to interact today in a way they never could before, *commodities*, ideas, and attitudes all get *disseminated* with unprecedented speed. The latest fads—whether we're talking about electronic technology, clothing, perfume, fast foods, whatever—they now frequently become not just national but international, global phenomena.

That's one influence, air travel. Now another and maybe equally important influence has been the communications industries . . . um . . . which . . . and I'm going to include the Internet in that category, along with the media —TV, radio, newspapers, magazines, and film. We can't really discuss the subject of a global culture without considering the powerful influence of these things. Today, as we all know, film and television are multimillion, even billion-dollar industries. Films, documentaries, news and current affairs programs, quiz shows, even soap operas are usually made in the hope that they'll be bought and shown around the world. As a case in point, take shows such as *Friends* or *ER*. They're watched on every continent and have universal appeal, as they're based on universal human problems, on personal relationships and emotions. But these programs also present and promote ideas and attitudes. They enable viewers to see with their own eyes other ways of life. And, of course, an important element in all this is advertising. Let's not forget that the media receives most of its money from advertising—which means that advertising's a major feature of television, magazines, etc. Advertising works through the media, so we're constantly exposed to it and influenced by it. That's to say, the global spread of fads I mentioned earlier owes a lot to the power of advertising. So, just as, say, in the U.S. commercials proclaim that it's cool to wear Reebok trainers, that Kellogg's cereals are the healthiest way to start the day, that Colgate toothpaste gives your teeth the best protection, and so on . . . well, they're probably getting the same message in scores of other countries, with the result that, globally speaking, people's habits are changing; they're *converging*. What's an example of converging habits? . . . Oh, here's one. Many Japanese today eat cereal for breakfast rather than traditional rice and soup, or, uh, maybe have a hamburger at McDonald's for lunch. And, likewise, Americans or Canadians might choose sushi, tacos, or Chinese food. In fact, today most people, at least in large cities, expect to get almost any kind of ethnic food. The fact is that the media spreads ideas incredibly widely, quickly, and effectively—whether it's cell phones, eating habits, fashion, whatever—and that's what makes it such a powerful marketing tool. To understand just how powerful, think for a minute about the music industry. Consider how television, radio, newspapers, magazines, and the Internet have been used to promote music and pop stars internationally. Stars like Elvis, the Beatles, Madonna, Michael Jackson, Britney Spears, uh . . . the Spice Girls . . . these and other stars have acquired world fame, thanks mainly to the media. And the same is true of sports teams and stars. These celebrities are internationally famous, and people in different corners of the world want to imitate them, have similar lifestyles; indeed, that's why companies use celebrities to advertise their products. The idea is that if Ronaldo uses, say, Nike soccer shoes, then you'll want to do likewise, whether you're American, Argentinian, Korean, whatever. That's the message. And the result? Youth around the world end up using the same brands.

OK. The media, then, clearly plays a major role in spreading trends across the globe and *highlighting* our similarities. But there are other forces at work too, and world politics is surely one of these. Although political divisions and *ideologies* continue to separate nations, it is, I think, true to say that, generally speaking, that *prejudice* is *diminishing* and people are increasingly open to other cultures and ideas. To some extent this is no doubt the result of political and therefore social convergences, of unions such as the European Union which represents a group of countries with quite different traditions in many cases, but where, nevertheless, there exists a spirit of unity . . . or at least cooperation. Europeans are beginning to feel that they're members of a larger culture that's more than simply a political convenience. Heads of government increasingly appear to be consulting and acting together on issues that affect the world at large, such as the environment and third-world poverty. Because these things are reported in the media on news shows like CNN and are seen by millions, they create a sense of pulling in the same direction . . . a feeling that there's a "culture of humanity," if you like.

There's another way in which politics can affect the spread of ideas across the globe, and that is through controlling the movement of people across national borders—immigration and emigration. Political circumstances—as well as more accessible international transportation—have brought an increase in the number who choose to emigrate to another country. And when people move, so do their ideas and beliefs. Immigrants introduce things from their own cultures into their new communities . . . from sports to food, house décor, games, you name it. Again, in many countries, from Australia to England, we're seeing cultures mixing together as never before. This increase in cross-cultural contact—along with the decrease in prejudice I mentioned earlier—has led to many interracial marriages, which in turn have produced children who are familiar with more than one culture. This again reinforces similarity, the idea that we're all members of one human race, despite surface differences. As a result, I think we have a new global superculture that's both richer and more diverse than any one single culture.

Now, communications lie at the heart of most of the things I've been talking about. Even though air travel and the media have allowed us glimpses of each other's cultures, people could not *convey* their ideas, beliefs, and attitudes if they couldn't communicate them. So, what I want . . . what I'm trying to say is that I'd like to acknowledge the role English has played as the world's unofficial international language. If you want an example, just look at the Internet. In 1990 there were just a few hundred Internet sites; today there are tens of millions, and the vast majority of these are in English.

All right. Although I've only touched on a few very broad ideas, I'd like now to finish talking about the forces that are shaping a global superculture and end by briefly sharing a few thoughts on where this trend's going. I should first say that I think a global superculture's *inevitable*. And, in my opinion, in many ways that's a good thing, perhaps even an ideal. It emphasizes the oneness of mankind, promotes unity, and, I would argue, helps prepare the way for a fairer world where the earth's resources benefit everyone and wealth is evenly distributed. However, that is not to say that these things must be at the expense of cultural traditions, cultural diversity. Today, for example, we see the Ainu of Japan, the Chipaya of Bolivia, and the Penan of Malaysia on the list of endangered societies. If these and other cultures were to disappear, we'd lose the wonderful variety and richness of human life, whether we're talking about philosophies, clothes, or food. To some extent we'd lose part of what has made us what we are today, lose touch with our roots, perhaps even the variety and individuality that makes us unique as a species. What's more, there'd be practical . . . possibly very significant practical implications. For instance, we may lose the benefits of alternative approaches to . . . to . . . medicine, social systems, farming techniques, not to mention spiritual *insight* and the like. People in the developed world not only have a lot to give, but also a lot to learn from other societies about these and other things. We're already learning that technology doesn't necessarily bring advancement; it can also bring destruction, materialism, and a decrease in morality and social cohesion. And what about the purely aesthetic representations of human civilizations; what of art forms? Do we really want to lose the rich variety of art traditions, the many different cultural expressions of human existence. Perspectives on problem-solving too—dealing with environmental issues, say, creating a balance with nature—may be lost to us. Wouldn't these losses be tragic? I, for one, believe that future generations need to incorporate insights from a multitude of cultures. This would perhaps go some way toward preserving those cultures and traditions which very simply make human society richer and more colorful.

OK, well I could say a lot more but, as always, time doesn't permit. So, to summarize then, we've looked at some of the main factors that are contributing to an emerging global culture. They include, at least, cheap available air travel, the enormous power and influence of the media, changes in the political scenery— exemplified by the European Union, perhaps—and the role of English as an international language. I started by asking whether these developments will mean that individual cultural traditions will inevitably disappear. The answer, I think, is that, sadly, many already have, but it's possible for others to survive. For this to happen, we need to think more carefully about the potential dangers of globalization, as well as its benefits, and we need to appreciate the value of these traditions, for only then will we think twice about carelessly losing them. Let's just hope enough of us realize that before it's too late.

OK. In preparation for your essay, I'd like you to think about ways in which we can ensure the survival of cultural traditions in a world where a superculture is rapidly emerging. Are there any questions?

Unit 12 Computer Security

TEACHER: All right, why don't we get started here. I'm quite sure that everyone in the class uses a computer regularly. For instance, uh, who uses e-mail every day? Right, just about everyone. Uh, how many of you use the Internet, say, at least five times a week? The same, just about everyone in the room. I think we would all agree that our lives have been changed and in many ways improved by the computer and the Internet; however, there are real dangers here. The fact is, computers and computer networks have created opportunities for crime that never existed before. As a result, the police and justice departments are becoming increasingly concerned about the growing number of computer users who are *accessing* private or secret information. Now this problem is on the increase worldwide. Statistics are showing a trend toward more computer crime every year. In fact, recent studies have shown that around 70 percent of all companies that are online have experienced some type of attack. We can say that there are three reasons for these dangers.

Now first, personal computers hold huge amounts of information, and some of it's quite sensitive. Companies have sensitive business information, new products, and financial records to protect. Governments have defense secrets, federal banks, and records for millions of citizens. We've found that the theft of information is usually financially motivated. Some companies try to get information from their competitors by accessing information from computers. Computer criminals also access and steal information in order to sell it to other people or competing companies. Again, their purpose is usually financial gain.

OK. In the first case, the criminal steals information and then possibly sells it. The second reason for computer crime is to steal money directly. Banking, insurance, and business organizations use computers for most of their transactions, making them the hardest hit by computer criminals. Now think about this for a moment. The American banking system alone *transfers* over 400 billion dollars every day. With this amount being transferred daily, it's no wonder that experts fear that a major financial disaster could occur.

Now you may be interested to know that between 1 and 3 billion dollars are lost each year in the U.S. through computer crime, and 40 percent of large American companies suffered at least one major instance of computer fraud in the last ten years. Can you imagine? Forty percent! We can see from these figures how serious a problem this is. I call the people who commit these crimes computer criminals rather than hackers, because hackers may not be motivated by financial gain.

Now this is how a typical *scenario* might go. A computer criminal—um, let's call the criminal a "he"—figures out how to get into a bank network. He changes account names and numbers and puts money into a bank account that he has already opened. He then withdraws the money from the account, which is of course not in his real name. His crime has just made him rich.

In case you were wondering, this has actually happened many times in the past. In companies, goods can be stolen and inventory, that is the list of goods, and sales figures can be changed to *cover up* the problem. Mailing addresses can also be temporarily changed so that expensive or valuable items are sent to the criminal's address. The accounts can then be changed back to the original addresses. Sometimes they don't *detect* this type of robbery for months or years, so it's impossible to find the criminal because the records have been changed back. Now remember—these things are not just stories; they have really happened.

All right. Let's consider the third reason for computer crime, which involves hacking, that is, breaking into someone else's private computer network, often that of a company or agency. Now hacking can take place for various reasons, but it tends to be done by individuals, not organized groups, and those individuals are typically young men in their teens or twenties. Some apparently do it for the challenge, while others feel angry at society or feel powerless in their everyday lives. Hacking provides such people with something they can't get elsewhere—an exciting and complex challenge, an opportunity to show how much they know, and a sense of importance.

Now that we've considered some of the causes of hacking and computer crime, let's consider the effects. Well, the events that have occurred in the past twenty years are astonishing. On more than one occasion, computers all over the world have been shut down as a computer virus has raced around the planet. In less than twenty-four hours, billions of dollars in work hours have been lost. Computers in major companies, and even major software companies, have been shut down completely. In one case, approximately 70 percent of the computers in several European countries were shut down. Even government computers were affected. How can this happen? Easy—the *transmission* of a simple virus program. Even beginning students of computer science can make powerful viruses that can do everything I've just mentioned. They can write a virus program and send it via the Internet to hundreds of computer users. The virus enters the user's computer's operating system, replaces good files with a copy of itself, and then sends itself to other computers *via* the computer user's e-mail address book. Soon millions of computers can be infected.

Now there's a whole other side to this problem that is more closely related to your life. Imagine that a computer criminal is able to get, um, let's say, your credit card number. In the best case scenario, this will cause you a great deal of inconvenience, and in the worst case scenario, it will cause you financial loss. Another possibility is that someone may get your social security number; then they can impersonate you. This can lead to serious problems and huge costs in terms of time spent solving the problem and the stress involved. The more powerful a technology is, the more potential there is for problems.

Well, I've tried to give you some background about the seriousness of the problem, but now I'd like to briefly talk about the battle between hackers and computer criminals on the one side and the people and companies interested in preventing these problems on the other. What's being done to stop computer crime? First, the courts are getting much tougher with hackers—the people who illegally enter a computer network—even if they claim not to be stealing anything. The courts are also now punishing computer criminals more severely in order to give potential criminals a strong message that computer crime is serious, and if you're caught doing it, you'll be punished. Some of these criminals have gone to federal prison for several years and been fined large sums of money. This is seen as a way to discourage people from experimenting with this new type of crime.

Now within a company or other organization, firewalls are the first line of defense—the first way to deter computer crime. A firewall is a software program that acts as a gatekeeper between the Internet and a company's intranet— that's I-N-T-R-A-N-E-T—the network of computers used by the company's employees. Now one type of firewall examines the source address and destination address of all of the data going in or out of the network. It can stop some data from entering the network and other data from leaving. However, firewalls can't protect networks from all attacks. In the past, hackers have often gotten around a firewall by accessing the network from a modem that an employee has brought in on his or her own without talking to the system administrator. Such employees are also trying to find an easy *route* around the firewall, usually because they want to access data on their work computer from home. These paths must also be closed, so if you have a *colleague* who is doing this sort of thing, you should definitely talk to them because they're opening a door for potential hacking.

And another way to increase security is through the use of less obvious and less easily remembered passwords. For instance, employees are often advised to never use a person's name, such as "Nancy." Here's why. Many hackers use programs that are called password guessers. These programs check every word in a large dictionary, all of the names in an encyclopedia, and then they use each entry in a local telephone book. As you can guess, if you have used almost any word in your local language, the hacker will eventually find out what it is and then be able to get into your system. The most difficult passwords to guess are a combination of small and capital letters, numbers and punctuation marks, such as "capital Y, zero, three, exclamation point, small M." Try finding that with a password guesser. In addition, passwords should be told to the minimum number of people.

OK, a fourth method concerns access-control software— something which has become quite common. Now this software limits the user's access to information as well as the operations he can perform. So for example, access-control software might only let people read certain files or programs but not input data, and it may keep them out of other files entirely. Many universities use this type of software. Computer system administrators at the school can access the entire system; teachers can access a great deal of it, but not as much as the system administrators; and finally, students can access fewer areas than the teachers. It works on a "need to know" or "need to use" basis. Encryption software has also been developed to *scramble* data so that hackers can't understand it even if they do steal it. The data can be read and used only if the user knows the key. Now this is a very effective way of protecting information. Encryption has developed rapidly since the 1980s, so now all of us can have access to fast, affordable, and powerful encryption systems. These systems are already resistant to the average hacker, and in a few years only government or military supercomputers will be able to break most codes.

And finally, audit trails—that's A-U-D-I-T trails—are also available. Audit trails monitor the use of a computer and alert owners to any attempts to enter their computer system. It's usually possible to identify any user who gains access to the system and when the access occurred, making it possible to trace the hacker. Although this isn't simple to do, it can be done, particularly if the hacker *persists* and returns for repeated attacks on the system. One way that some hackers have been caught has been when the system administrator has what is called a "jail ready." Valuable-looking but false information is put in the jail. This might be something like credit card numbers or other sensitive financial data. When the hacker tries to get the false data, the administrator uses software to determine where the hacker is. The software follows the line of data back to the hacker's computer.

Well, those are some of the major things that are happening at present to decrease computer crime. None of them are completely satisfactory, but together they're certainly helping to maintain the *integrity* of personal and corporate computer systems and communications. And these changes, as well as the improvements that are certain to come, should influence people to stop hacking by making it less profitable and more risky. And this will help ensure confidentiality when communicating via computer. Well, let's stop here for today, and get started with your presentations. Our first speakers, uh, Carlos and Yumi, are scheduled to talk about encryption. . . .